Now I

I feel that God put me in a place
Where my own emotions, I would now face
I obeyed God when He said to take pen in hand
Words He would give me, soon the reason I would understand
So, as God gave me the words I began to write
Words so real, they showed me the light
They showed me the pain and suffering I was holding inside
Was shared also by others whose loved ones had died
So it was for myself and others, words releasing our feelings and emotions
That these poems were written with both love and devotion
I thank my friends and all my family
For their encouragement and the belief they had in me
But, without God and the words that He spoke
These words in poem I would not have wrote
For my book is filled with words from our Birth until our end
In between how we lived our lives and came to depend
On the ways of others, slowly losing sight
What we were doing wrong, not wanting to make it right
So, in writing my book, it clearly seemed
To call it, from Birth to Death and Life In Between
It was because of this, yes, my book was born
Now, I too am tired and my body feels worn
But, I obeyed God, and once again pen and paper I took
To write and give to you my last book
From Birth to Death and Life in Between

Words in Motion

From Birth, to Death, and Life in Between

Written by:

MARLENE SCOTT

authorHOUSE®

AuthorHouse™ LLC
1663 Liberty Drive
Bloomington, IN 47403
www.authorhouse.com
Phone: 1-800-839-8640

Published by AuthorHouse   04/04/2014

ISBN: 978-1-4918-9850-5 (sc)
ISBN: 978-1-4918-9861-1 (e)

A CAT'S MEOW

I became friends with a man in the house I was in
I followed him everywhere, right to the end
One night he got drunk tried to cut out my eye
Then he buried me behind this wall to die
He then brought in another cat to take my place
Got drunk again, tried to kill his wife and cat, what a waste
He buried them too, with me, behind the wall
Not knowing the police would soon be called
Neighbors heard our scratches and meows
When the police arrived he cried foul
But, then they heard us behind that wall
They got us out, said thanks for the "Cat Call"
He forgot we cats have nine lives, so, he is doing time now
We got our justice, thanks to a CATS MEOW

A Childs' Prayer

I watched as this young boy came to the altar today
And my heart broke as I heard him Pray
Dear God, I am not asking this for me
I am asking this for my Mommy and my Daddy
Please touch them and heal their pain
I want them to come back to church with me again
God, I know that you know just what they need
And God, you can use me to help plant the seed
You gave me to them to give them happiness
And I really am trying to do my best
Every day I give them a hug and say "I love you"
Then wait for them to say that they love me too
His head still bowed as he arose
I saw his tears as down his cheeks they flowed
God, please cradle him in Your arms when he goes to bed tonight
Let him know that you heard his prayer, things will be alright
For you said that the little children will suffer not
And God, I know this child you have not forgot

This little boy did come to the altar that Sunday and prayed for his parents
I was sitting close to him and I heard his prayer to God

A DAY in the LIFE of a MOTHER

I have so many errands today that I must run
I'm already tired and I have just begun
I must taxi the children, taking them to school
But on the way, I have to pick up a little friend or two
Then, grocery shopping, that's next on my list
Checking it twice, to make sure there is nothing I missed
Back home, I now must do the laundry, clean and dust
Put something out for dinner, that is a must
Whew! Done with all that, and just in time
Back to school to pick up the children, I hope just mine
They do not like to stand around and wait
So, I must hurry, I dare not be just a little late
Well, here we all are, finally back at home
Children said they are leaving, saying I needed to rest, a little time
alone
But, they said they would be home for supper, it can be a surprise
Make it quick and simple, like hamburgers and fries
The day is now almost over, everyone is in the sack
I am going to sit in the tub and relax
Get some rest, for me morning comes early, another busy day
But, if anyone asks me why I do it, I will have to say
Every day that I am with my children I discover
That whatever I do, it is not work, but it is called love, part of being a
Mother

A Mother Makes the Family

A Mother will face many a trial
While trying to raise her beloved child
But of all the jobs, there can be no other
That has the joys and rewards than that of being a Mother
She gets no pension, nor can she ever retire
Her job is guaranteed, she cannot even get fired
From the moment that her child is born
She will never leave them, even when she gets tired, grows old or
worn
She tends to her child through all their years
Leaving with them memories of laughter, joy and tears
Yes, a home may have a Father, a sister and a brother
But, it is not a family unless there is Mother
Mother, when I too grow and have a family
I pray for all the those things you instilled in me

A PASTOR

A Pastor is someone in whom we can trust
A Pastor is someone who is true and just
A Pastor is someone who always cares
A pastor is someone who, our burdens he will share
A Pastor must walk that extra mile
Though he is tired and worn, must still have a smile
A Pastor knows that he too must sacrifice
If he is chosen by God to have Eternal Life
We have such a Pastor, always near by, close around
Ready to pray for us if we are sick, feeling depressed or down
He will answer our call no matter the day or time
Saying, "yes, I'll be there, no, I do not mind"
When he preaches, he is always on fire
Especially when preaching God's word and telling all the Devil is a
liar
He loves to sing loud, to the Heaven's above
Letting everyone know that God is indeed, his first love
Our Pastor has a wife and three young sons
Who stand behind him and the work he has done
His family supports him as we also do too
We say "thank you and yes, we love you"
Yes, Pastors may come and Pastors may go
But this one thing I surely do know
That Pastors, it is true, there are many
But there will never be another Pastor like our Pastor Kenny

**WRITTEN FOR OUR PASTOR, PASTOR KENNY GRIFFIN
OUR FIRST AND ONLY PASTOR OF OUR CHURCH
LAKESIDE OUTREACH MINISTRIES**

A Smile Remembered

I want to tell you about this beautiful "child"
Who has the most captivating smile
Her smile will lift your up if you are feeling low
Staying with you, no matter where you go

I was on my way to our church Revival
When suddenly my day became one of self survival
It seemed the Devil fought me the entire day
Wanting me to do every thing his way

I was very tired and upset, but I still went
To our Revival in our Church, some called a tent
When I entered, a peace came all over me
I knew the presence of God was there, indeed

I was being greeted by each and every one
As I heard the song that was being sung
I quickly took my seat, and I became transfixed
By the power of God's music with the family of Rick's

I heard the voice of Lester and Earl and God's spokeswoman, Eloise
Singing and praising God's name so AWESOMELY
But, there was one who stood out, and when she looked my way
She smiled, a smile that said, God has been with you today

Her name is Gloria, the name they told us
But I think that God calls her, ANGEL GLORIOUS
I know God sends His Angels in some form and some way
I know God sent the KINGS CRUSADERS to us all that day

A Weekend/Long Overdue

This is the weekend, I will have some fun
I'm going to the mountains with my beloved son
We seldom get time to be with each other
Due to work, sometimes illness or even the weather
But, here we are today, all ready and set to go
And a good time we will have and share I know
It's not often that we get to have quality time
But God gave me this weekend, said it was mine
We will use this time, just my son and me
We're going to the mountains and just be carefree
God said, "enjoy this time that I have given to you
For this time together is long overdue

WRITTEN FOR JOHN

Aging Gracefully

Well, I'm getting older, wrinkles I have got
Along with a few extra pounds, well, maybe a lot
My hair is slowly becoming gray
And you can guess what else is beginning to sway
A hearing aid I definitely need
Bifocals too, if I want to read
I have a cane to help me walk
Adding to the embarrassment, my dentures loosen when I talk
A double chin I have, it looks like I'm trying for three
Wow! it sounds like the years have got the best of me
But no, now just hold on
I may be older, but, I can still have fun
I still go dancing, out on the town
A little slower perhaps, but I can still get around
I can jump and holler as loud
As anyone else in a crowd
True, I may need to sleep a little longer
Exercise more to help my bones grow stronger
My memory, now that is the best part of all
Many years stored up, happy memories I can now recall
If I could reverse this aging process
How far back I would go is any ones guess
Life has been good to me, many blessings, yes a lot
I have friends and memories that will never be forgot
A family that loves me and really cares
A husband, many memorable years together we have shared
With all of this, I am proud to stand up and say
I am now a Senior Citizen, hurray, hurray

ALL ALONE and BY MYSELF

As I sit here, all alone, again tonight
Something just does not feel right
I feel warm and cozy beside this glowing fire
I thought being alone was really my desire
I just wanted to have peace and a little quiet
Just once, I thought I would try it
But being alone is not what I expected it to be
The only one I can talk to is ME_ME_ME
So, I'm picking up this telephone
Giving someone a call, please come over, I'm all alone
I'll keep the fire burning, all aglow
So hurry on over, I'm waiting, don't be slow
You're here already, now things feel right
Thanks for coming, I needed the company tonight

ALL I WANT
{to my children}

I want no flowers, no jewelry, none of that stuff
That some think in giving is thanks enough
You can buy me a new outfit, yes, you could do that
Even add to the outfit a new pocketbook, shoes, and hat
Or, you could send me on a much needed trip
Maybe even a cruise, across the ocean on a ship
You could take me to a movie {I may have already seen}
Take me out dancing, called making the scene
All these things are nice and in good taste
But for me, it is money spent, almost a waste
For all I want is for you to find time to spend with me
Come by for a visit, have dinner, or a cup of tea
To give me a hug, a kiss, to just keep in touch
Tell me you love me, now is this asking too much?
Today, I will be sitting by my telephone
To get that call, saying, "Mother, I'm on my way home"
Put the coffee pot on cause I am on my way
To spend time with you, this Mother's Day

America Welcomes You

We believe in helping our fellow man
We believe in doing all that we can
We believe everyone deserves the chance
To better their lives, their futures to enhance
But, we also believe that we have the right
To defend our country from all who might
Cross our borders, into our land with only one thing in mind
To cause dissention, hatred and mistrust in all mankind
But, it will not work here, for America is strong
You will be found out and sent back to where you belong
It is true some really do want to start a new life
Free from fear, threats, prejudice and strife
So, they sneak across our borders, trying to get in
In hopes of a new life they want to begin
It is only the ones who want to rob and kill
That causes the people to say "we've had our fill"
Then our wanting to help them turns to hate
Demanding we send them back before it is too late
Yes our country is open to all who want to be free
But we will not let you take away our Liberty

An Anguished Prayer

Lord, you have laid upon me such a heavy load
And I find myself walking down a long and rocky road
But every time I thought the end was in sight
I began to stumble, wanting to give up the fight

But then I would hear Your soft and gentle voice
Saying, "it is now your time, you have to make a choice"
You can lay there weakened, without hope, be in despair
Letting the Devil win by telling you that no one cared

Or you can get up, take My Hand and stand tall
Believing that with Me beside you you will not fall
For I will show you the light at the end of the road
And I will lift from you this heavy load

Yes, sometimes the road is long, but there is an end
Where you will find a renewal of life at the Rivers Bend
For once you travel this road others will follow unafraid
Like Me, they will know the sacrifice for them you too have made

Yes, I have let you walk the road and I have showed you the light
So that you may guide others, giving to them an insight
That if they too want to make Heaven their home
They must travel that road, with Me your will never be alone

So give Me your burdens, reach for and hold my hand
And I will lead you to the Promised Land
No more pain or sorrow or darkness of night
For I will carry your load and show you the light

AN OPEN LINE

WHEN I AWAKE HEARING THE BIRDS ALL SINGING
I KNOW IT IS GOD SAYING, "WAKE UP, YOUR PHONE IS
RINGING:
I AM CALLING YOU TO SAY, "I LOVE YOU AND TO LET
YOU KNOW
I WILL BE WITH YOU ALWAYS, WHEREVER YOU MAY GO"
I'LL HOLD YOUR HAND AND GUIDE YOU THROUGH
WHEREVER YOU GO, WHATEVER YOU DECIDE TO DO
YOU HAVE A DIRECT LINE TO ME, IT IS CALLED PRAYER
JUST USE IT, ANYTIME OR ANYWHERE
YOU WILL NEVER GET A BUSY OR AN ANSWERING
MACHINE
SAYING LEAVE A MESSAGE, I AM AWAY FOR THE TIME
BEING
I ANSWER ALL MY PRAYER CALLS, ONE ON ONE
I AM ON CALL, 24-7, MY WORK IS NEVER DONE

ANGELA

The aches and pains, oh how our hearts cry
When a loved one leaves suddenly, no chance to say "good-bye"
Then we find ourselves all gathering together
Trying to understand and to comfort each other
Angela left behind a daughter and a son
She was so proud of them and what they had become
She also left behind a brother, Donnie, she loved him so
Although at times, she found it hard to show
Angela was a person who was very loving and caring
She did not have much, but she was always sharing
The birth of her grandchildren was the highlight of her life
They gave to her much love, made her forget a lot of her strife
Although Angela knew she was loved by many
She still fought demons she felt had become her enemy
She truly fought hard, wanting her pain to cease
Crying out for help and praying to God to give her peace
Angela was very, very close to her Mother Faye
And it left a void in her life when her Mother passed away
Angela, God has now given to you the peace you asked for
He is now uniting you with your Mother that you so adored
Though all your loved ones here are now crying out
For answers that has left them with so much doubt
You will be missed Angela, memories our hearts will retain
And know that a part of you in all generations will now remain
We are all comforted to know that you are now at peace
Peace you prayed that one day God would let you reach
We know your Mother Faye will be standing at Heaven's Door
Her arms outreached saying, "my daughter, welcome, you will suffer
no more"

ANGIE

When I saw this ring upon your finger
I thought, I hope she does not wait or linger
To marry the young man who placed it there
His way of committing to you and saying "I care"
I know that you are really hesitating
But I do not know why you are waiting
When God took the love of your life home
He never intended for you to be alone
You both served God and loved one another
You both vowed you would always be there for each other
It was your beloved that God chose first
Leaving a void and a heart that hurts
But he would want you to go on with your life
Saying it would be a lucky man who chose you for his wife
God's richest blessings upon the two of you
When you walk down the aisle to say, "I Do"

**WRITTEN FOR A WONDERFUL FRIEND OF MINE WHO
LOVED HER HUSBAND VERY MUCH
THEN GOD TOOK HIM HOME AFTER A LONG ILLNESS,
NOW, SHE HAS FOUND SOMEONE WHO LOVES HER
AND WANTS TO MAKE HER HIS WIFE**

ANGIE

There were some things I still wanted to say
Things that I tried to say, each and every day
You always gave so much to me, but asked for so little
Sometimes I know you were caught up in the middle
I wish I had carried more of the burdens that worried you so
But, I always knew you would say "God will take care of it, let it go"
Then I learned as the years rolled on to leave the past behind
I began to see my Blessings and I found that God indeed was kind
God showed me that even clouds cannot banish the Sun
And the world will look better when God's work is done
God said that the heart suffering from the hardest trial
Becomes the purest joy, yes, God's rewards makes all things
worthwhile
Angie, I know you are going to be alright and someday you too will
see
The purpose God had for you and for me
I promised you a home on earth, you waited for it so patiently
God promised me a home if I too believed
Angie, God said together on earth we did have a home
Where we shared our love for God and were never alone
A family we raised, made sure they knew wrong from right
Prayed God would watch over them and they would be alright
One day, I know you will find another that will win your heart
And together, a new life you will then start
Go with my Blessings, and yes, with my love
Know I will continue watching over you from above

**ANGIE, I TRULY BELIEVE THAT THIS ACHING HEART OF
YOURS GOD TRULY SEES
AND GOD SAYS YOU ARE FREE, AND YOUR JOYS ARE
ABOUT TO ME
WRITTEN FOR MY SISTER IN CHRIST, ANGIE GRIFFEN
WORDS I FELT COMING FROM HER BELOVED HUSBAND
JOSEPH {J.C.} GRIFFIN WHO PASSED AWAY TWO YEARS
AGO**

BAD HAIR DAY

My beautician, while trying to do my hair
Kept answering the phone, with understanding and care
To a caller who was really having a bad time,
Wanted an appointment, but could not make up her mind
Can I get an appointment with you today she would say,
I have a ride, they are on their way
I do not know what time I will be there
But please, I need you to do my hair
I have no car, so I must solely depend
Upon my family, or call a friend
And if they cannot come, then a taxi I will take
Cause my hair looks awful, for goodness sake
I'm coming today, time wise I don't know when
But know I will be there, please, just squeeze me in
I want the works, shampoo, cut, and set
Then I will feel better, on that you can bet
My beautician set down the phone, then looked at me
Saying, that was a customer saying they were really in need
I knew she was frantic when I answered the phone
I could tell by her voice and the tone
I told her it sounded like her hair was really a mess
I told her, come when you can, I will do your hair, yes, yes, yes

BEAUTIFUL LADY

Such a beautiful lady, such a beautiful smile
Always willing to go that extra mile
She will always listen, care and be concerned
While telling us that some things in time we would learn
But she would listen then tell us to do our best
To put our trust in God, He would do the rest
She said in this world in which we now live
We must also learn to forget and to forgive
What a wonderful lady, who has God's special touch

HAPPY BIRTHDAY MS. JANE, WE ALL LOVE YOU VERY
MUCH

THIS WOMAN INDEED IS BEAUTIFUL, SHE HAS MS AND
IS WHEELCHAIR BOUND, BUT, SHE IS ALWAYS SIMILING
AND I HAVE NEVER HEARD HER COMPLAIN, WHEN I
SEE AND TALK TO HER, SHE MAKES MY DAY AND I AM
SO BLESSED TO HAVE COME TO KNOW HER

WRITTEN FOR A SPECIAL LADY THAT I HAVE BEEN
BLESSED TO COME TO KNOW
I ALWAYS SEE A SMILE ON HER FACE NO MATTER
WHAT . . . SHE IS A BLESSING TO HER FAMILY
AND ALL HER FRIENDS . . . GOD BLESS YOU ALWAYS, MS.
JANE

Because I Let God In

This morning I awoke with great anticipation
I was waiting to get out of my bed
I no longer was afraid of any temptation
Because I knew God was with me on the road ahead

Somehow I just knew that on the darkest day
The Sun, most surely would shine
I only needed to let God lead the way
I knew God was more than just a friend of mine

God has never left me He is always by my side
He has always filled my empty heart
So today, I knew my prayer would not be denied
As I cried out, "oh God, how great Thou art"

Today God has sent me on a path
That will indeed, change the rest of my life
I will meet a friend who will again make me laugh
Someone who will help me forget my pain and strife

God, I give thanks and praise to you every day
For your love and for filling my empty heart
I now know if you do not let God in, or open that door
You will never find the peace and love that you are searching for

BEWARE of UNWANTED LOVE

You told me that you loved me and that you cared
But, when I needed you, you suddenly were not there
You wooed me with flowers that you would send
But, I now find out that it was all Pretend
For me, yes, I felt I really did love you
And I thought that you loved me too
My love was real, but yours was not
But, from this experience, I have learned a lot
I shared with you my love, my secrets, my pain, my trust
Because you said, our sharing together, was a must
My heart is now aching, it is truly broken
But, time will heal this hurt, now I have spoken
I wish you well as you go your way, you have made me aware
Not to freely give of my love to someone who does not care

IRENE, I TRULY BELIEVE THAT SOMETIMES A TRAGEDY
LETS US JUMP INTO WHAT WE THINK IS A SOLUTION,
AT THAT TIME ANYWAY, WE GIVE OUR LOVE, OUR
TIME, OUR SECRETS, FEARS, AND ALL, AND THEN FIND
OUT IT WAS NOT THE ANSWER WE WERE LOOKING
FOR . . . . STEP BACK, YOU CAN STILL HAVE FUN, ENJOY
LIFE, BE YOURSELF AND DO THINGS WITH YOUR
FAMILY, FRIENDS, AND LOVED ONES, BUT, DO NOT
LET ONE THING DOMINATE YOU . . . . GOING OUT TO
CLUBS, HAVING A DRINK OR TWO, THINKING YOU
ARE HAVING FUN, THAT IS NOT AN ANSWER, THAT IS
NOT A FUTURE . . . YOU HAVE A FUTURE, DO NOT RUN
DOWN THE ROAD TOO FAST WANTING TO SEE WHAT
IT IS AND TRY TO GET IT BEFORE IT IS TIME, WALK
THE ROAD SLOWLY, CAUTIOUSLY, AND WHEN YOU GET
THERE, YOU WILL BE READY AND IT WILL BE THERE
WAITING FOR YOU

TAKE CARE OF YOURSELF IRENE, ENJOY YOUR LIFE, YOUR FAMILY, FOR NO ONE CAN LIVE THIS LIFE FOR YOU, YOU MUST LIVE IT YOURSELF, KNOWING YOU HAVE GOD, TRUE FRIENDS, FAMILY, LOVED ONES HELPS US THROUGH EACH AND EVERY DAY . . . GOD BLESS

******BILLY******

Billy had finally found a wonderful home
Where he felt welcome, no longer alone
Years of loneliness was all forgotten here,
Where he lived happily for many years
The girls also felt God had sent him their way
To help ease their burdens they had from day to day
Billy never felt uncomfortable as the only "Mister"
In this home dominated by women, everyone knew was the sisters
Billy was a quiet, gentle man who loved God and life
He brought calm to all when he felt any strife
It was here that he found a "Soul Mate" in Sister Bea
Proudly telling everyone, "she means the world to me"
But, God called Sister Bea home a year ago
Bringing sadness to all, again, Billy's loneliness began to grow
Billy became sick and he prayed for God to take him home
Where he knew he would never again be alone
So God in His mercy took Billy home to be with his soul mate
Where they would meet each other again, at Heaven's Gate

**IN LOVING MEMORY OF WILLIAM ALLAN HICKMAN
PASSED AWAY JUNE 24TH, 2013
HEAVEN AWAITS . . . FOREVER**

Blue Monday

Here it is Monday, some call it Monday Blue
But for me, I hope that it is not true
I pray that today, all things will go smooth
They say that all good things come in twos
When I awoke this Monday morning, I looked outside
I heard God say, you have choices, take time to decide
You can either complain or make do
With thing that come your way and are handed to you
Remember, if you have legs and feet, you can walk
If you have a voice, then you can talk
There are many who cannot see or hear
Many living as a shut in, because of some fear
But they do not blame others, saying it's the fault
Of someone else or punishment for what God has wrought
Instead they take each day, thanking God for being alive
Saying, "I have overcome and I will survive"
Say, today, Monday, is just like any other day
I will trust in God that I can do whatever He sends my way

BONITA

The words are truly hard to find
To express to you at this time
You have felt heartache and much blame
Feeling your life would never again be the same
But Bonita, know your loved ones have felt your pain too
Wanting to help carry your burden because they love you
Your faith in God has taken you this far
You will make it, you are strong, yes you are
Bonita, I would just like to say
As you remember your loved ones today
Your cousin Kevin and Earl, your brother
Just remember that they are now both together
Together in a place we too one day want to be
Forever with God in Eternity

OUR PASTOR'S WIFE WHO BURRIED HER BROTHER AND
WATCHED HER COUSIN DIE IN A CRASH
ALL WITHIN HOURS OF EACH OTHER

**Written for Bonita who lost both her brother Earl Miles and her cousin Kevin within
A few days of each other . . . Dec. 2012**

Bonita/Crystle

Hello girls, I know it has been a long time
But, I know I am still very much on your mind
Know that I am still watching over all of you
And God is also keeping a record of all you do
Earl my son has since left to come be with me
He said this was where God now wanted him to be
Tell Raven that her memories of me keeps us close and in touch
And that I love her very, very much
Keri my precious, there are good things for you waiting
But, it is you that just keeps hesitating
You must grab hold, your future must go on
You cannot give up on life and say, it's over and you're done
God says that if we just believe
Blessings from Him, we will receive
Crystle, such a hard worker, holding the family together
Your nieces and nephews think of you as a friend, their Aunt, their
Mother
With two beautiful daughters, your heart they both have won
Your life with them has just begun
Bonita, I now know God had chosen you to be
A preachers' wife, working for his ministry
And if you could only see what God has in store
You would be knocking harder at God's door
I saw what happened to Kevin that day
Bonita, I ask God to let you hear what I am going to say
Man thinks he has plenty of time, God says, "not so"
Only He knows when it is time for man to go
So it was on that fateful day
It was God, not you who caused Kevin to go away
Sometimes we must all carry our burden throughout the years
When we will question God and cry many tears
God says trials we must sometime endure, before on Him we call
But, He will hold our hand, He will not let us fall

I have seen all of you walking with God, then stumble a bit
But held on to you, saying, "no, not yet"
Your Faith walk with God has now become stronger
And your fear of falling is no longer
To all my grandsons, Corey, Dustin, John and Duane
Your future is your making, no wrong turns, stay in God's lane

My granddaughters, Raven and Keri, you make quite a team
Little spats here and there, but not as bad as they seem
If one needed help, the other would be right there
You are sisters, loving sisters who really care
Kenny, your struggles have been many and long
But, it is your faith that have kept you and your family strong
Thank you all for being my wonderful family
By the way, I see it has increased by three
Always by your side . . . love you

BRIANNA

Golly gee, you are growing up way too fast
I want to keep you a little girl, as long as it will last
I want to see you run and play, being a playmate
To all your friends and with your brother Blake
You are such a cheerful, loving child, yes, you are
And you are wiser than your age, oh yes, by far
God made you special then gave you to us
Knowing the love you would give to all you would touch
You have a Mommy and Daddy that loves you so
Every day is a Blessing, as we watch you grow
Grandmas, Grandpa's, aunts, nieces, cousins, just to name a few
That love you so much and will always be here for you
You have a MEME, she is one of a kind
The two of you have a special bind
Today, we have all gathered to help you celebrate and to say
We love you Brianna, have a HAPPY, HAPPY BIRTHDAY

BROTHER DONNIE COLLINS

He spread God's word, whether written or spoken
His promise to his God, he had never broken
Whether on the street, in church or on the roof top
He would spread God's word nothing could make him stop
So many souls have made it to Heaven's Streets if Gold
Because Donnie preached to them God's word and how he too was
made whole
Donnie was a gentle man, so respected and very much loved
But, he took no credit, said all he was He owed to the Man above
Respectful of others, whatever their needs, He prayed with them all
Was always ready to go where he was needed and called
He believed that we were all God's children, treated everyone as such
Made sure that everyone knew God and how to stay in touch
Yes, He delighted in his journey, and at the end of his life's path
It could all be summed up, HE WALKED WITH GOD, a simple
epitaph

PEACE COMES AFTER SUFFERING, LOVE THE REWARD
OF PAIN
THEN AFTER EARTH COMES HEAVEN, OUR LOSS,
HEAVEN'S GAIN

Brother J.C./Remembered

We have all gathered here today in your name
Where we will celebrate your birthday, by playing your favorite game
A Tractor Pull, your other love, your favorite pass time passion
Participation with family and friends, it gave you much satisfaction
However, your first love and passion was in doing the work God gave
to you
And nothing kept you from doing what He had told you to do
God said to build a church, where we could lift our voices and sing
And you committed your life to this one last thing
Then when God it was time to go, you knew
You would be leaving in peace, having done what God told you to do
The impact that you left on all those you met
Will remain with us always, you, we will never forget
For our love for you did not die when you passed
You are etched in our hearts, forever it will last
Your dream you started is still being carried out
The building of our church, it will grow, we have no doubt
Your determination, hours of sweat and tears, your labor of love
Was not measured in money, but knowing your reward came from
God above
That is why our church will continue to grow, and one day in time
We know you will proudly look down from Heaven saying

"LOOK GOD, LAKESIDE OUTREACH MINISTRIES, THAT
CHURCH IS MINE"

HIS SON, OF WHOM HE WAS SO PROUD IS THE PASTOR
OF THIS CHURCH
REV. KENNETH GRIFFIN

BROTHERS

We took a trip the other day
One that was really far away
We drove from the early hours of dawn
Finally pulling upon my brother Buford's lawn
He met us outside with open arms and a cheerful smile
Making this long trip really worth while
He then called our brother Tad who too
Was awaiting of news of our arrival from our brother Boo
Boo called Tad saying, "our brother Royce is finally here
Let's meet somewhere to eat and talk about family and yesteryear
So, we all met, along with Shirley, Tad's devoted wife
Who has helped him overcome so much sickness and strife
A delightful person, smiling at the stories told, taking it all in
Saying, in some of that, I wish I had been
They laughed and talked, so many memories were shared
By these three brothers who showed each other how much they cared
Another day of memories and togetherness they will now recall
While waiting for that next visit or telephone call

WRITTEN FOR THREE WONDERFUL BROTHERS,
THOUGH THEY DO NOT SEE EACH OTHER A LOT NOW
DUE TO DISTANCE, BUT THEY KNOW THEY ARE NEVER
FORGOTTEN AND ALWAYS IN EACH OTHERS HEART . . . .
GOD BLESS YOU ALL
BUFORD . . . TALMADGE . . . ROYCE
SCOTT

California Recall

I do not live in your state per say
But I hear about you and your happenings, everyday
You are in the papers and all over the news
About your Governor, a new one you want to choose
You want to recall one and put into power
An actor, a name known by all, a man of the hour
The only Body he has tried to build
Was his own with the American Guild
You elected a Governor, Davis, Gray
Now you want to remove him, take him away
All because you say your state debt has risen
And for no other reason have you all given
You forget that a debt is not made by one man alone
So let's cut to the quick, get right to the bone
If you really wanted a TOTAL RECALL
Then you must get rid of them all
The man who started this whole thing
Was because he wanted to throw his hat into the ring
All this could have been settled by vote in a year or two
Now, look at all the monies that this is costing you
Don't let armatures come in and make fools of you
Even Arnie knew that one time was too few
He had to finish his job in TERMINATOR TWO
Arnie is well known for his roles and movie fame
Recognized by all, you just need to say his name
But, this is not a movie or a casting call
Casting a vote, will affect you all
The taxpayers have to pay for this recall
For someone who may not last at all
It is a temporary solution that is only made worse
It's like a Doctor having to work without a nurse

So, choose you actor if you want him to be
The star attraction on your government marque

But, if you want to keep your government in tact
Then vote for someone who knows all the fact
Say, "Austin-la-Vista" to all who would like to be
The next Governor of your great state—Californ-i-e
It reminds me of the Gold Rush in "49"
Everybody rushed to get there, but it took time

**Written in Aug. 2003 when Arnie decided to run for the
Governor of California**

CANCER . . . THE ANSWER

I never knew the day would come when I would hear
The Doctor say "I'm sorry, but, you have Cancer I fear"
He gave me words of comfort, telling me what I now must do
Assuring me he will be right beside me to see me through
I now must go and tell my loved ones and my family
I must give them comfort and assurance, while they also comfort me
We are strong, a family of faith and love for each other
And we will face the days ahead together
To my family please just remember one thing
With God things are not always as bad as they seem

CANCER . . . THE ANSWER . . . OH YES
IT'S CALLED PRAYER . . . MEDICINE AT IT'S BEST

Choosing our words Carefully

We must be careful in the choosing of our word
For once they are spoken, they then have been heard
We cannot then take the words back
By saying, "I am sorry, just give me some slack
Even if spoken in a rage or a moment of outburst
Regardless, they are cruel words that can hurt
Yes cruel words often are quickly spoken
But still, they leave many with a heart that is broken
God gave to us a voice that we could use
But to express ourselves, our emotions, not to abuse
Words can be given for comfort and to give praise
Words of kindness can really make ones day
Give to others words of love that shows your emotion
And the words can also expresses ones devotion
WORDS . . . choose them wisely, they must be sincere
WORDS . . . of love and respect are words we all long to hear

COLTON

Hi Colton! I visited you in your school today
I walked softly down your hallway
I stopped at each room that I passed by
Just wanted to look at my children and say Hi!
Some rooms were so quiet, but some were, well,
Making so much noise, they did not even hear the bell
Many children Colton, that day I seen
Most were very nice, but some were being quite mean
They were showing off, trying to flex a muscle or two
On several of the students, including you
Colton, some children flex their muscles because they cannot admit
That it is really they, who are the misfits
Tomorrow they will look back on all this and say
What happened to me to make me act that way?
If I could see that student today, I would shake his hand
Tell him I am so sorry, forgive me, I did not understand
I know it is hard to understand, but know all are being tested
Especially the children in whose future I have invested
It is how we behave now and how we treat each other
That will one day give us understanding and bring us all together
Colton my son, you are nervous now I know
Even at times feeling inferior causing you to be a little slow
But, you have been chosen so for that day you will be prepared
Know I will be with you always, do not ever be scared
I will walk the halls with you every day
When someone tries to bully you, just smile and walk away
That high hill you see but feel that you must climb
Yes Colton, you will make it to the top, it will just take time

Written for the grandson of my friend, Alice Ballinger

COST of the CROSS
JESUS PAID THE PRICE

They tried to take away our Jesus
But, He had made a promise He would never leave us
They tried so hard saying that at any cost
They would nail our Jesus to the cross
They thought that forever He would be doomed
When they crucified Him and laid Him in the tomb
But, on Easter Sunday, this is the day that we were given
As the day that from His tomb, Jesus had arisen
Into Heaven to His Heavenly Father He would then ascend
But with the promise to us He would one day come back again
He said we would not know the day or the hour
That we must never forget His love or His power
That we must live each day as Jesus wants us to
And be prepared for that day when He comes for me and you

Crossing God's Border

Every time we see or hear of a new baby being born
We should all be happy, but why do some of us mourn
Is it because they look at this new life, about to begin
And see them being thrust into a world of greed and sin
Our world has become so insensitive to the need of others
That we no longer consider ourselves, or call each other, sisters and brothers
Their future and their learnings, should be taught to them in our schools
But, they are not being taught to learn and to obey the Golden Rule
Instead, they are told who to sing about and to idolize
And to punish or hate the ones whose rules they defy
They are told to sit back, do nothing, only to complain and to whine
For they are being taught to freeload off others, saying, what is yours, is also mine
They feel they do not have to work, but just sit back
Letting others work harder to take up the slack
Our people need to be taught to stand up and fight
Do not let the Government give them handouts and say, it's alright
We fought for their freedom and their right to speak
For without freedom of choice, we become weak
We need to put God and religion back in our churches and schools
We need to stop letting a minority make us look like fools
Our young people have turned to violence, robberies, killing whoever they can
Trying to put a scare into, and to intimidate their fellow man
One day, God will say to all those in Government power
Your day has now come and this is will be your final hour
Jesus said He died and suffered so His people would not
He now needs to let my His people know He has not forgot
So to those of you using your power I say, get your own house in order
For you have defied me, you have now crossed over into My Border

CRYSTLE

You have gone far above and way beyond
Working hard every day, from dusk to dawn
Taking care of not only your own family
But also my very own, just like you took care of me
You have kept your promise to our Mother
That you would take care of us, keeping us always, together
Though sometimes differences caused us to drift apart
We still remained close, always in each others heart
I know that you still feel my presence around
Since God came to move me up to higher ground
Crystle, you now too must move on with your life
Being a good Mother and yes, a good wife
They all need you so very, very much
Wanting you to give them your all, and your loving touch
So, look around you and enjoy your life
Fill it with happiness and love, not with strife
For one day at peace we all will be
When we meet again in Heaven, where forever we now will be

**Written for Crystle after her brother Earl passed away, she was
and still is a symbol of strength
In not only her family, but being there to lean on, talk to and
help in all she can for the children
Of Earl.**

Dedication

Thank You God
God, I thank you for this day
I thank you for all that may come my way
I pray for Your guidance in all that I do
God, let me live my life so others see you in all I do
I may not be perfect, but You know I try
I have good days and bad when I laugh and I cry
I laugh with happiness wherever I see God's Blessing
I cry in sadness when I see among our loved ones, tempting and
testing
God, this day I ask for, though it is not just for "I"
But for everyone who will receive and I know you will not deny
For I know the Blessings you have given to each of us
Is because you have no favorites, but you love us all very much

Don't Look Back

I know God says "don't look back"
Yesterday has passed, that's a fact
Do not dwell on what could have been
Remember, it is God on whom you must depend
God did not say that we must put aside
Our loved ones who have died
But we should hold them within our heart
Remembering each generation is not a past, but a start
Take care of each other, our loved ones would say
For though we have moved on, we will all meet again one day
Take pride in all that you set out to do
Because the way you live your life, reflects on you
Keep God with you, always by your side
His love for you is unconditional, it cannot be denied
Keep your promise, stand firm In what you believe
One day God's promise to you, you will receive

DREAMS

Yes, dreams are a fantasy, they are not real
They let us dream of how we would like to feel
We sometimes find comfort by just closing our eyes
Dreaming of things that our life to us has denied
We can hold up a love or that special someone
Looking for happiness and bliss, under the moon, the stars and the
sun
Living out your fantasy because you know that when
You awaken, and you open your eyes, reality begins to set in
But dreams can also be an off set
To help us block out the things that we want to forget
It brings to us a calming, a way to relax
Helping us to deal with the life and the real world of facts
In a dream you are able to pick or choose
Whoever at that time, you want to be with you
And because this is your dream, your fantasy
You can do and make it whatever you want it to be
But please, do not just dream, for you must also face tomorrow
Remember, that in both dreams and reality, we face sorrow

EARL

Today we sat quietly as we all said a Prayer
Asking God the question, why, when, and where?
Questions that were asked by each of us
Upon the sudden loss of someone who was loved so much
Today we all stand before God, his family and his friends
Saying good-bye to a loved one whose life so quickly did end
Earl was a loving husband and Father and a devoted brother
Who only wanted peace in his family and for them to love one
another
Yes, Earl would sometimes vent, speak his mind then smile
Saying, "we kept it in the family, that makes it all worthwhile"
When Earl first met Lynette, he knew he would ask her to be his wife
He knew he had found his love, the love of his life
Two beautiful daughters, Raven and Keri, he deeply loved
Thanking God every day for the blessings from above
Corey was his chosen son, he came to love so much
Wanting that special bonding of a Father's touch
Two sisters, Bonita and Crystal, yes, they were very close
He was so proud of them and of them he would often boast
Nieces, nephews, cousins, aunts, uncles, he loved them all
Prayed daily that they would all be ready when Jesus called
A near death experience made Earl realize that God had given him
more time
To be with and near the loved ones he would soon leave behind
Earl had problems, failing health, but, he faced them, he did not run
He said, "I have faith in God, if it be His will, it will be done"
Kenny, his brother-in-law, their closeness could never be denied
Earl knew he had Kenny and God always by his side
Pastor Kenny was always there for him, no matter the time or day
With a warm embrace, to listen, to talk, or just pray
Earl was like a gentle giant, strong but willing to give his all
Loved his God and wanted to be ready when he was called

We know Earl was ready when God called him home
He will always be with us, he never left us alone
As God takes you into the Promised Land
There, your loved ones and your Mother wait
To bring you through Heaven's Gate
Today, we do not say good-bye to Earl, a man we all adored
You will always be remembered until we meet again, on Heaven's other Shore

**WRITTEN FOR THE FAMILY OF
EARL MILES
12/05/12**

<u>EMILY</u>

I know you found the perfect prom dress
Fixed your hair, wanting to look your very best
For prom night is such a special night
Bringing with it, excitement and much delight
Being escorted by that special someone with whom you care
Giving you memories that you both will share
They should have voted you both, King and Queen
For you had to be the loveliest couple to be seen
So, Emily, we just want to say
We love you, have fun on this, your special Prom day

FAULTS?

Uh-Oh! You said that I had a fault
OK, I admit it, I guess I got caught
I'm very impatient, this I will admit
Especially with people or things I'd like to forget
I'm also a heavy drinker, this is true
I drink lots of coffee, yes, more than a cup or two
When I get nervous, I bite my nails
And I love going to lots of yard sales
I also tend to stay up pretty late
Taking care of things I could do tomorrow, but can't wait
But, come morning, I do not sleep in
I am up early, cup of coffee, ready for my day to begin
But all in all, I truly believe
That I am me I do not try to deceive
I try to be honest, help anyone, whenever I can
If I see a wrong, I'm not afraid to speak my mind or take a stand
I also believe in God and doing His will
By living for Him and to show everyone that my God is real
Yes, I've lived a long life, and I may be getting old
But, deep down I know that in my Soul
God never found a fault with me
And His is the only opinion that I need
We all have faults, God has forgiven mine
He steps in when I get impatient or out of line
So, if I have offended someone over the years, to you I say
I am sorry forgive me, now, LET US ALL PRAY

FINDING MYSELF

A SLEEPLESS NIGHT, SO MUCH ON MY MIND
MY SANITY, I AM TRYING HARD TO FIND
TAKING ON THE PROBLEMS OF SO MANY
TRYING TO FIND ANSWERS, I DON'T SEEM TO HAVE
ANY

YES, I WANTED TO BE A GOOD NEIGHBOR AND A
FRIEND
SOMEONE ON WHOM PEOPLE COULD DEPEND
I WANTED TO GIVE THEM COMFORT, A NEEDED WARM
EMBRACE
TO HELP THEM THROUGH THINGS, WE ALL ONE DAY
FACE

BUT IN TIME I BECAME TIRED, I FELT I WAS LOSING
TOUCH
ALL BECAUSE I CARED AND I TOOK ON TOO MUCH
I ALWAYS FELT NEEDED, ALWAYS IN DEMAND
I IGNORED ME, AND THINGS JUST GOT OUT OF HAND

MY FAMILY MY FRIENDS, YOU ALL DID KNOW
THAT I WAS ALWAYS THERE FOR YOU, ALWAYS READY
TO GO
BUT TODAY GOD TOOK MY HAND AND SAID, I'M
STEPPING IN,
YOU NOW NEED TO FIND YOURSELF, AND TO YOURSELF
BE A FRIEND"

I WILL TAKE SOME TIME TO LOOK INSIDE OF ME
FIND THE ANSWERS AND WHAT GOD SAYS WILL BE
WHEN I GET THE ANSWERS AND THE PEACE WITHIN
I WILL THEN BE BACK, I PROMISE YOU MY FRIEND

Finding Time for Jesus

We always seem to find the time for all the things
That it seems like it fills our busy day
But just how much time do we allow
Whenever it comes time to Pray

Jesus just wants what is best for us
He does not want what is leftover, or feel used
For He deserves a place over and above
All the things that we so often choose

So, if we will start each day upon our knees
With only Jesus being on our mind
Then we find peace, our mind will be free
Our rainy days will soon be filled with sunshine

For it is only Jesus that can bring us joy
A joy so unspeakable and so true
But only if we will find time to spend with Him
Can He find the time to spend with me and you

FIRE

I never thought of FIRE in this way
That Rev. Mitch preached to us one Sunday
He said it was our love for God that we should luminate
By spreading God's word before it is too late

That if we are on "FIRE" for our Lord
And our Souls are all of one accord
Then we should spread God's word
Fanning the fires so they can spread and be heard

God's word should be as a Fire that cannot be put out
Though it may flicker at times when we have a doubt
We should all believe and all remember
That the Fire will burn brightly as long as God is the EMBER

BROTHER MITCH PREACHED THE WORD OF BEING ON
FIRE FOR GOD AND WE SHOULD ALL KEEP
THE FLAMES BURNING BY SPREADING GOD'S WORD
AND NEVER LETTING THE FLAMES GO OUT

Follow Your Heart . . . It knows

God said He watched the other night
This young girl so bewildered and full of fright
He said she was confused on which way to go
As into adulthood she continued to grow
Yes, I have watched this young girl, so very carefully
Each day, I see her drawing closer to me
She feels as though she is so alone
But, no longer wanting to find reasons to roam
She still does not full realize
That I see her pain and I hear her cries
I have seen her come to the Altar, kneeling in Prayer
Crying out my name, God, please show me that you care
She needs to know that she is very much loved
Surrounded by Angels from above
She is young but I have given her time
To get to talk to me and to clear her mind
She needs to keep praying and reach out to me
Then I will show her how she can be free
Experiences are okay if from them you will learn
But some experiences, it is best to spurn
My child I have plans, there is a future for you
If you will follow me, your heart will tell you what to do

Frances Elizabeth Williamson
5-17-1949-----8-21-2013

An illness this loving, caring lady fought for so long
Although she struggled, her faith kept her strong
Frankie was a loving Mother, raising her children in hopes one day
she would see
All her children serving God and raising their own family
Frankie did get to see all her children become grown
Seeing each of them getting married, having children of their own
She beamed with pride as she held each and every one
All eleven grand, three great grands, but still praying for more to
come
She held them close to her heart, each in a special place
Thanking God every time she seen their smiling face
Larry, her loving husband, always in her heart and by her side
They had a special bond that could not be denied
Four daughters, Tammy Christine, Cheri and Lynette
All are left now with only memories of a Mother they will never
forget
Then, the day came when she heard God say, "I have come for you"
A peace came over her, for she now knew
That God had touched her, taken her by the hand
She was now ready to be taken to the Promised Land
Do not cry for me, I have loved ones who now
wait
To welcome me Home as I enter into Heaven's Gate
And I know right in front, waiting with them all
Will be Earl Miles, my very special son-in-law
My final wish is please from God do not ever stray
For I want to see all my loved ones again one day

FRIEND to FRIEND

I called you often, I talked to you
Asking if you needed anything, was there anything I could do
I told you I was someone on whom you could depend
I had a shoulder to cry on, if you needed a friend
One day when I did not call you or stop by
I heard that you sat down and cried
I heard you said I was not there when you were in need
And that you were very upset with me
But, did you ever wonder if I were okay
Or think maybe, I too may have had a bad day
Maybe I needed someone to listen to me
Because, I am not perfect, I have problems too
If you have a friend who really cares
A friend who tries her best, who tries to share
As much of her time that she possibly can
Doing it all willingly, sometimes on demand
Just remember that friendship is a two way street
Somehow, somewhere in the middle, both must meet
For if one day, she should not call or stop by
Then, you go see her, give her a hug, and just say "hi"
Then she too will feel a friendship that has grown
Because friends do not let friends be alone

FRIENDS FOREVER

My love for you has now passed
We knew it was a love that could not last
For we are of two very different worlds
Who just got caught up in a romantic whirl
You had your ways and I had mine
We could not change or leave the past behind
I truly pray that you will one day meet someone
Enjoying your life together, for life can be fun
Our time together was great while giving us the time to see
Where we were going and what we wanted to be
We both tried to walk that long, long road
But, each step we took, became a heavier load
I now have found and I hope you have too
That special someone, meant for me and for you
Know you will always be special to me, a real good friend
Friends forever, a friendship, I hope will never end

<u>FRIENDS</u>

Please, do not dream, dreams of me
Because dreams are not what one really sees
You are reaching out to touch someone who is not there
To keep on dreaming and wishing is not fair
For waking up brings to light the reality
That it was only a dream that can never be
I really do not know what else I can do
I have always tried to be honest with you
If I have misled you in any way
I am truly sorry I do not know what else to say
To me a friend is someone in whom you can confide
Dry your tears when you are sad and cry
Someone who will listen to your every word
Making you feel better, knowing you were heard
Someone who comes to your rescue when in need
No questions asked, just saying, "you can count on me"
A friend is unlike a Love that is lost when spurned
A friend asks for nothing in return
Yes, I am a FRIEND, not a dream or a fantasy
And a FRIEND is what I want to be
So, if you are asking about you, my heart and how I feel
I see you only as a very SPECIAL FRIEND who is very real

FROM LOVE to FRIEND

The day that we first met
Is a day that I will never forget
God brings some of us together for a reason
Just like our weather too has a season
Sometimes our love ran hot and then cold
Just like Autumn leaves we too change as we get old
But in between the Winter/Spring and Fall
There is a Summer, lots of love and warmth, that says it all
Then just like seasons, changes we too began to see
That only friends we soon would be
We were bonded by children born out of love
Children God sent to us from above
To be the parents He knew we would be
Yes, He made them to be a part of you and me
In time, our lives changed just like the weather
But, we have a bond that forever will keep us together
Maybe no longer a strong love, this change I regret
But you will always be a friend that I highly respect

From Old to Bold

Now I know Doctors are important to us all
Even if they no longer will make a house call
Instead they make you come, sit and wait
But, they get mad if you are just a few minutes late
They take you back look you all over and before long
They ask you the question, "what seems to be wrong"?
Well Doc, if I knew, I would not be here in the first place
Complaining to you about all my pains and aches
Well, he says my body is getting older, it is all tired out
You must start slowing down, there is no doubt
Your blood pressure today is sky high
You could easily have a stroke and die
Your liver, well it doesn't look so fine
Better stay away from the alcohol and wine
And your lungs, you are wheezing and short of breath
Those cigarettes will surely be the cause of your death
You are a little overweight with those extra pounds
You should be in a gym or out jogging around
Your eyes, you could see better if you had glasses
You have cataracts starting to form in great masses
Your heart cannot take much more strain
So, from everything you like, you must now refrain
"Well" I told the Doctor, "I'll make sure your bill gets paid
It will be part of the will I am having made
So, I left his office, went home, feeling really down
Then I thought, okay, one more time I am going to do the town
So I went out and I danced all through the night
Didn't come home until broad day light
Yes, I was tired but happy, I had so much fun
It had been years since these things I had done
And you know what I discovered?

It may take my body longer, but, I will recover
So, I intend to enjoy the life I once had

Stop trying to find things wrong and be glad
Glad that I am alive and can still do things, although
I may not be as agile and my body may be a little slow
I will keep on enjoying life until the day I die

Doing all the things the Doctor told me to deny
Doc, I took your prescription to stay healthy and live long
I did everything you said for me was wrong
You cannot imagine how happy it has made me
No more waiting rooms or Doctor's fees
So Doc, if you feel that I need to see you again
Call me, make me an appointment, I'll be back, I just don't know
when

FROM THIS DAY FORWARD

TODAY WAS THE BEGINNING OF A WHOLE NEW LIFE
WHEN BEFORE GOD, WE WERE PRONOUNCED,
HUSBAND AND WIFE
THIS MEANS THAT WE WILL LOVE, HONOR AND OBEY
NOT JUST FOR TODAY, BUT FOR EVERY DAY
TOGETHER OUR HOME WILL BE FILLED WITH LOVE
AND LAUGHTER
BEGINNING NOW AND FOREVER AFTER

CONGRATULATIONS TO THE NEWLYWEDS, MAY YOUR
NEW BEGINNING ALSO BE A BEGINNING WITH GOD
BLESSINGS FROM PASTOR KENNY
&
LAKESIDE OUTREACH MINISTRIES/KENNETH GRIFFIN
MINISTRIES

Fulfilling Our Urges and Needs

When I was younger I chased after the flesh
But, as I got older, I found I had to get more rest
Yes, I slowed down, but I still
Had the urges and a satisfaction I needed to fill
My body says my wants and urges I have kept confined
But they sure are addictive they keep preying on my mind
I understand it all and if the truth be known
It is just that I am tired of now being alone
So, one day I started thinking when I started feeling blue
And the urge took over me, now what was I supposed to do?
So, I went out looking, yes indeed
I was trying to find someone who could take care of my need
As fate would have it, someone came along
She tuned my piano, she played my song
Together we found harmony and bliss
We sealed our undying love with one long kiss
I am happy now, as happy as can be
Because I now take care of her and she takes care of me

GILA BEND . . . MY ROCK

Gila Bend, what a beautiful place
To sit and ponder, and memories to embrace
Memories of family outings, just being together
Brother/sister . . . Father and Mother
Though our children have all grown and moved away
We still stay in touch, most every day
They also still go back to sit and reminisce
About our loved ones gone, we all truly miss
A son/brother, a wife and loving Mother
In our memories here, but in Heaven together
So, when I return to Gila Bend . . . my Rock
I smile and my heart rejoices as I turn back the clock
Yes, Gila Bend holds memories, here I find peace
God willing, these visits will never cease
For when I need comforting, I can always depend
On the peace and serenity at GILA BEND

GOD IS TESTING OUR FAITH

It is true that monies are needed for overhead
But, even in an empty field, your sheep need to be fed
We all need a place to gather praising God in voice and song
It is a place where all who come, get along
God gave us a church, He answered our call
Now we are being tested, to see if we will fall
GOD said we should not close our door, if only for one
Walking through that open day may be the soul that is won
But, the faithful will remain, yes we will
Until again, our church we will again fill
So GOD, we will gather every Sunday to worship and pray
We all have faith, and yes God, we did it Your way

THIS WAS WRITTEN WHEN A DECISION WAS MADE TO
OPEN ANOTHER CHURCH WHEN THE ATTENDANCE
ON SUNDAYS DROPPED SHARPLY, HOWEVER, OUR
PASTOR STILL REMAINS FAITHFUL, OPENING OUR
CHURCH DOORS EVERY SUNDAY, EARLY SERVICE TO
ALL THOSE WHO STILL COME WHILE STILL PREACHING
AT THE NEW CHURCH

God/Through the Eyes of A Child

God is good and God is kind
God helps us all to stay in line
God sent teachers to set up a Sunday School
God said that we need to obey the Golden Rule
God kicked Adam and Eve out of Garden of Eden when they
sinned
God told them to never come back there again
God let David take down a Giant with a sling
And for being obedient, He let him become a King
Then, when Daniel fell into the Lion's Den one day
God showed him how to get out if he just prayed
He healed the sick and made the blind to see
Gave strength to Samson so the slaves he could free
He parted the waters so people could then cross
They wanted their freedom, no matter the cost
God got mad because of sin, said He wanted a new start
So, He showed Noah how to build the Ark
He let it rain for 40 days and 40 nights
God destroyed everything that was left in sight
However, God knew that before things could be complete
He had to do one more thing, His hardest feat
God knew He had to give up His only Son
To suffer for us, if His will was to be done
God is awesome, God is so great
God is always with us when needed, He is never late
Even as a child I know that no matter my need
It will be done if I but let God lead
God, I am so sorry for all your suffering and pain
But I know if needed you would do it all over again
You say a child sees no wrong, he trusts and believes
That a child is innocent the day they are conceived
God, when I hear or speak Your name, it brings a smile
I thank You God, for letting me be Your child

GROWING OLD

Yes, the years have finally taken their toll
And I know this body is getting old
Some are quick to say in words not so kind
She can't remember things, she's losing her mind
But this mind holds many memories I hold so tender
So many memories, yes, I still remember
For this mind was once young and very sharp
Stored memories, I still carry in my heart
Some things can never be taken away
Like remembering to talk to God each and every day
It is God who has brought me through so very much
He will call me home when He is ready, He is in no rush
Although you are giving up on me and rushing me through
God says the decision is His it is not up to you
These words you remember that to you I now say
We all get old and you will too one day
One day your time too will come
To stand before Jesus Christ, the Father, the Son
We will not be judged on our age or year
Or be asked if we remember why we are here
God will simply say, you remembered to do My will
Now to you, My promise I will fulfill
Welcome home, my faithful one
Your work in earth is now done

GROWING OLDER/GRACEFULLY

When I was a teen and growing up
I liked to listen to rap and all that stuff
I even thought that I was really cool
Dancing around the dance floor acting the fool
Well, I know I will not see "21" again
I see my hair is beginning to thin
I used to be active, but I have found
That it is harder for me to now get around
And my hearing, though I still have an ear
The sounds are not as audible or clear
And if that is not enough to add to my grief
The Dentist said I have to lose all my teeth
Even my peepers, getting harder to read
Those thick horned rim glasses I will soon need
It may sound like my whole body may be shot
That it's all over for me, but guess again, it's not
Some may even think that I am not all there
But I know some one who really does care
He will love me no matter how I look
His name is Jesus He has my name in His book
He said I would age and grow old Gracefully
One day, with Him, I would live an ETERNITY

HELLO EARL

Hello Earl, we just wanted to say,
You are being remembered, on this, your special day
This is the day God placed you here on this earth
It was then called, the day of your birth
Then every year thereafter, upon this date
We would all gather with you to help you celebrate
But then one day, God called you home, you were reborn anew
And a new birthdate was then given to you
When God called you home on that day we will not deny
It was too soon for us, we miss you, and yes, we still cry
Today, we are again gathered to celebrate and remember you
Knowing that in Spirit, you are here with us too
We are sending up to you our love, and we want to say
Celebrating with the Angels in Heaven, now that is a
BLESSED—HAPPY BIRTHDAY

Written for the family of Earl Miles who left us so suddenly this year . . .
Today would have been his birthday, and he is remembered by so many
of his family and friends

HELLO MOTHER

Hello Mother, you came into my mind today
As I sat with my children, watching them play
It brought back so many memories of yesteryear
Memories I have kept and held so dear
As I started traveling back on memories lane
I kept seeing your smiling face, I never heard you complain
No matter how busy you were, you always had the time
To sit with me and listen to what was on my mind
You encouraged me to do my best in school
And you supported me in all that I tried to do
I also remember that sometimes, when things for us got rough
You were there with your love, to us that was enough
I smiled as I remembered watching you when you cooked
And I kept thinking of how beautiful you looked
I found myself hoping that one day, I too
Would become a Mother, just like you
Then with your Blessings, when I became grown
I left my home to start a life of my own
I soon married and started my own family
I want to be the Mother to them, that you were to me
Every time I hold them or give them a kiss
I will see you holding me, those times I truly miss
When I take them to the beach, walk in the sand
I will remember how we too walked the beach, hand in hand
When I go to their school or to the PTA
I will see you there too, as if it were only yesterday
I have them now for a while, but one day I know
That I too will be giving them my Blessings to go

To begin their own families with their memories to share
Of a Mother who loved them and truly cared
Memories are great, but children, please do not wait

Tell your Mother how much you love her, before it's too late
For there is nothing that will ever compare
To the love that a Mother and her children share

HER FUTURE TAKEN

When I first heard about this story
Of a young girl who loved her country and OLD GLORY
So much so, she was in hopes one day to be
A representative in our Congress, representing, you and me
She delighted so much in all that she could do
Was very popular and active, especially in her school
She was thrilled when she was asked to go see
Another much loved, newly appointed Senator, they called "Gabby"
Senator Gifford also showed that she cared for us and was concerned
So, many things from her, this young girl had hope to learn
But, little did she know that on this day
She would become known, affecting the people, in a different way
She brought tears of sadness to the world around
Her lovely face and sudden death, kept us all spellbound
In her own way, though it was not by choice
She spoke to all of us, with a silenced, now muted voice
I feel that she would have asked all of us
To take this tragedy to bring us closer together, more in touch
Becoming more aware of how we speak to or treat each other
No longer as enemies, but, as sister and brother
Remembering that God touches all our lives in some special way
But, that for each of us, a different path He has laid
Yes, on this day, her dreams were shattered, her young life was taken
Leaving us all, angry, stunned, and shaken
Her dreams, our dreams, the dreams of our future generation
Can only be, if we learn to stand together, as one NATION

**I WROTE THIS FOR THE LITTLE GIRL WHO WAS SHOT
AND KILLED IN AZ
WHERE SENATOR GABRIEL GIFFORD WAS TO SPEAK
AND SHE HERSELF WAS SHOT**

HOODIES

Hoodies, yes, they are okay just as long
As you do not wear them to promote wrong
Hoodies are meant to keep us warm, especially our head
Not to be worn as a statement, like someone said
We should not be judged as to who we are
Whether it be by race, religion or by those from afar
People sometimes judge us by the clothing that we wear
But they do not know us or want to take the time to care
Clothing, just like Colors, should not be worn to be a factor
To hide from the truth, to do a wrong, or used as a distractor
Yes, Hoodies are comfortable they are warm and they look cool
But not to be worn as a symbol, or cause you to act like a fool
Can you wear a Hoodie? Yes, that is your right
But, don't wear it looking for trouble or to create a fight
When you meet someone on the street, tip your hoodie smile and say
hello
This is how we learn to trust and a friendship will surely grow

I Always Have Time

My friend, I always have time for you
No matter what you need me to do
When you are in need, you just need to reach out
Just give me a call, or just give me a shout
If you are ever sick and you need someone
Just call on me, you know that I will come
My schedule I can always adjust to find the time
To help out a friend of mine
You are a friend and you know I care
So, if you need me, just call and I will be there
God said an appointed time He has for us all
When we are needed, upon us He will call

I Cried out to my Jesus

JESUS, JESUS, I cried out your name
Crying, please tell me, am I to blame
Was it my sins that caused the loss
Of your life when they nailed to the Cross?
So many tears I have cried whenever I see
Just how much you suffered for me
Please God, show me now what I can do
To become more worthy of you
I now know the suffering you did for me
Was so that one day I too would be free
Yes dear Jesus, my life to you I now want to give
So one day in Heaven, with you forever, I will live

I overcame/You can Too

I try hard not to think of what may have been
But of where I am now, where I am going and when
Living on the streets or in the slums
Is where some of our lives had begun
This is something which we did not yearn
When opportunities arise, grab it, don't wait your turn
I am now concentrated on me as number one
I am no longer a loser, I fought the battle and won
I now feel like a person, a living human being
I got my chance to be free and clean
Yes, some of my friends I have left behind
Our lives are separate but they remain on my mind
I wish them well and I truly pray
That they too find their future and will be okay
For me, I found God and I no longer have to hide or run
For I know that in God, all trials in life can be overcome

I Will Get Through It

As a little girl Mother you tried to instill in me
To be true to myself and to be carefree
To go to church and to always Pray
For guidance to face any challenge that came my way
Growing up Mother, I watched you face hard challenges too
So, Mother, I know I got my strength and courage from you
I now am faced with a challenge within my own life
That is filled with lots of pain, suffering and strife
But, I know God is with me every moment of every day
With Him, I can face whatever comes my way

IF GOD BROUGHT ME TO IT
HE WILL BRING ME THROUGH IT
Written for my niece April who was just told she had Cancer

I WILL OVERCOME

I awoke this early morn with such a chill
And I cried out, "dear God, what is this that I feel"?
I feel that before this day is over and done
There will be a happening that I must overcome
So God before I put my feet on the floor
And start walking toward that unopened door
Please take away my fears and hold my hand
For only you know what's ahead, my fears you will understand
I know that with you beside me all the way
I'll be prepared for whatever that door opens for me today
And when I lay me down to sleep tonight
I will thank you for making everything alright
And when I again awake in the morn to start a new day
I know with you, I will overcome anything that comes my way

I'LL BE OKAY . . . THANK YOU

As a little girl Mother, you tried to instill in me
To be true to myself and to be carefree
To go to church and to always Pray
That I could face any challenge that would come my way
Growing up Mother I watched you face hard challenges too
So Mother, my strength and courage I got from you
I now am faced with a challenge within my own life
That involves a lot of pain, suffering and strife
But, you taught me to believe and I can truly say
I believe God is with me, no matter what comes my way

Written for my niece April to her Mother, my baby sister Michelle
Upon finding out about her Cancer . . . there is so much love, faith
and bonding
together within this family

I'M SORRY

TO MY LOVED ONES, I SEE SO MUCH PAIN AND
HEARTACHE
I KEEP ASKING MYSELF, "WHAT WILL IT TAKE"?
TO EASE THIS BITTERNESS AND WIPE AWAY THE TEARS
FOR I DO NOT WANT THESE PAINFUL DAYS TO TURN
INTO YEARS
I KNOW I DID SO MANY THINGS WRONG
I ADMIT, I WAS WEAK, I WAS NOT STRONG
I SHOULD HAVE TRIED HARDER DURING MY LIFE
TO HAVE BEEN A BETTER MOTHER, A MORE LOVING
WIFE
WITH ALL MY HEART, I ASK FOR YOUR FORGIVENESS
AND YOU TO KNOW
THAT I DID, AND I DO, STILL LOVE YOU ALL SO
MY HUSBAND EARL, WHO LOVED ME
UNCONDITIONALLY, I REGRET
I CANNOT ASK FOR YOUR FORGIVENESS, BUT YOUR
LOVE I'LL NEVER FORGET
TO MY FRIENDS AND FAMILY WHO HAVE STOOD BY ME
"THANK YOU", I AM TRYING TO CHANGE, YOU WILL SEE
TO MY CHILDREN, COREY, RAVEN, KERI, I KNOW THAT I
NOW MUST
AGAIN EARN YOUR LOVE AND YOUR TRUST
I KNOW THAT IT WILL NOT BE EASY
FOR ALL OF YOU TO AGAIN BELIEVE AND TRUST IN ME
BUT PLEASE, WORK WITH ME AND THIS BATTLE WE
WILL OVERCOME
AND WITH GOD'S HELP, WE WILL BE A FAMILY, UNITED
AS ONE

SO PLEASE, WE ARE A FAMILY AND WE NEED EACH
OTHER
EARL LOVED US ALL AND HE WOULD WANT TO SEE US
TOGETHER

WRITTEN FOR LYNETTE MILES
APRIL 02, 2013

ILLEGALS----To what Country are you now loyal?

You sneak across our patrolled borders
Causing chaos within our own law and order
You cause anger and disruptions within our own land
Against those who vowed to protect us and to take a stand
You came across and then you laughed at us
Because you knew that we Americans are quick to trust
You say all you need to do is give us an "ole" sob story
And just pretend to love our flag, "Old Glory"
Yes, some of you do find work, but you take your money
From this, the country you call, the Land of Milk and Honey
And you send it back to help all of those
Who want to come here and of our laws dispose
Some say they are here let's give them their right and freedom to
speak
Even if it is turmoil within our own country they really want to seek
But, freedom here in this United States does have a price tag
Especially when you trample on, burn, or disrespect our flag
Freedom of the Press and the ACLU
Does not speak for the majority, but only a few
Everyone cannot have it their own way
Here in our country, the good ole, U S of A
I know if you were as verbal in your own land
And against your Government you chose to take stand
Then you would not need to cross our borders on the run
For you would be imprisoned, your nightmare will have just begun
So, do not bring us your problems, but we will pray
That you will find peace and live in your own country one day

IRENE

Irene, I just wanted to remind you and to let you know
That I truly, truly, did love you so
When we first met, I knew there would be no other
Even though some said that we should not be together
We married and we then became as one
You were my world, the moon, the stars, the Sun
Yes, God said this would always be, until death do us part
But, then, we would live on always, in each others heart
I can see your hurt and I can feel your pain
I hear you crying, wanting us to be as one, united again
Irene, you were the Mother of our children, my friend, my wife
You were my love and the reason for my life
When God called me home, He said He was not ready for you
For their was so much, still waiting for you to do
For our children's sake, you must stay strong
Teaching them about God and right from wrong
You too must now go on, and with another find renewed happiness
You have my blessing and my soul will be able to rest
For you are still young, so much for you still lies ahead
Do not live your life as though you too were "dead"
I love you Irene and I believe that you now know
We will always be together, in memory, in our heart and soul

IRENE

I was looking down from Heaven the other night
Looking upon loved ones, to see if they were alright
Suddenly, I was led to this home, I remember it so well
Then inside I seen someone looking so sad, even pale
Sitting in bed, looked like they were watching T.V.
But, she had her hands over her face, I wondered how she could see
Irene, I know you are counting, it has almost been a year
Since I left earth and my loved ones, to be up here
But, if you could see my new family, my new home
You too would be happy to know that I am not alone
To my children, Zack and Megan, I loved you so very much
Now, even in death, we still, in memory, stay in touch
Irene, my love, my wife, I have watched your sadness and your pain
But leaving earth was not a loss, for Heaven was my gain
God never gave any of us a set time to be down here
But, He did want us to help others, be faithful and of good cheer
I want you all to live your lives to the fullest, be all that you can
I will be there cheering you on, for I am your biggest fan
Irene, I miss all of you, especially your beautiful smile
So, know that I will stopping in again, just for a little while

**WRITTEN FOR IRENE EVANS AND TO HER CHILDREN
WORDS OF COMFORT AND LOVE FROM KEVIN
BELOVED HUSBAND AND FATHER**

IRENE

There are things I still wanted to day
Some were things I told you most every day
We had our rough times throughout the years
I know many times I even brought you to tears
It was your smile, your laugh, your gently touch
That made me love, you so very, very much
At times you felt you gave so much and asked for so little
Sometimes we both felt we were caught in the middle
I wish I could help with the things that are worrying you so
But, I cannot, I am gone and you need to let me go
Irene my love, you need to know that I have set you free
No more sorrow or tears, you must stop looking for me
There is one more thing to you I want to say
It is that you fulfilled my life in every way
But, our life together as we knew it is over, it has ended
You are still there, but into another Universe, I have now ascended
God gave us our happy times together, but now you are again free
Being happy again is also a way of remembering me

**Written for Irene Evans who lost her husband Kevin, one year ago
Dec. 2012**

IT'S TIME WE HAVE OUR SAY

I have something that I want to say
About today, the start of a brand new day
Will it be about politics, scandals, or even me
Or about the war in some other country
It is so hard to obey the Golden Rule
Since our Government took Prayer out of our school
Our corporate scandals are getting so bad
They are taking away what monies the average American had
Even our elected officials turn the other way
When their own is found to be taking bribery and pay
We sponsor a war that many say is unjust
Costing lives and money, some call it Iran or Bust
They have no worry that it is costing us every penny
Those in the know are getting fat, the taxpayers are getting skinny
Our supreme courts are elected to be fair to us all
To speak for the majority, thereby enforcing our law
But, no, they chose to rule for the favor of some
So, where is the Justice, called, "one for all, all for one"
America need to get back on track
By putting Religion, Trust and Honor back
Back into our schools, elected offices and all that lack
The integrity and backbone, or having the spine
To stand up for what is right and not to whine
America means justice and being free
For every Americans, not just for me
Also, if you break our laws, then you must pay
For that is the American way
How about those immigrants crossing out border
And causing within our land, so much disorder
They take away the things that are ours
Like jobs and aide by using our justice power

To me the answer is very easy
As easy as saying, one-two-three
If you come here and you know you do not belong
You are breaking our laws, you know you are wrong
So, back you will go when you are found
We ask that our elected officials do not let us down
Because they get so busy, they want to appease
The countries you come from but are against us, you see
But, who do they call upon when they are in need
Good old America, the land of the free
We need to get back to being strong
And put US back in power where we belong
Freedom is ours, it is our choice
And with freedom, we have a voice
Our laws should be for the majority
Not for one or two or a minority
So let our voices all ring out
Stand up for freedom and to our leaders shout
We have elected you, so it is us you should defend
But, if you cannot, then the power we gave you must end

JUANITA

A family has gathered here today
Showing love, honor, respect to a loved one passed away
But, though there is much sorrow, there is also peace
Knowing her final destination she has now reached
Her own life was filled with stress and trials
But, she kept her Faith, with God she was never in denial
She knew He held her hand, was always by her side
Gave her peace and comfort when she cried
Children He gave her were a true blessing
Though God knew they would give her happiness, ease her stressing
So proud of her children, her grands and great grands
They loved her for who she was, they made no demands
Juanita, we know that you are now "countin"
The days when God will take you home, high on that mountain
When that day came and you reached the top
You knew you had made your final stop
It was there you would enter into Heaven's Gate
Where the Angels and all your loved ones now await
Juanita, "GO HIGH ON THAT MOUNTAIN TOP
YOUR WORK HERE IS DONE", it will not stop
You left behind a part of you and a legacy
That will live forever in love and memory

**WRITTEN FOR THE FAMILY OF A WONDERFUL WOMAN
JUANITA PARKER
HER SON RUSSELL SANG, "GO HIGH ON THAT
MOUNTAIN"**

A LITTLE "DAB" WILL DO YOU

I WALKED INTO THIS NEW, NEVER BEFORE SEEN STORE
THAT HAD A BIG SIGN, "MAKE OVER" OVER THE DOOR
SO, IN I WALKED AND I JUST KNEW
I WOULD COME OUT LOOKING OH, SO NEW
HE LOOKED ME OVER AND SAID, "I'LL TELL YOU TRUE"
MY WORK IS REALLY CUT OUT IN WORKING ON YOU
FOR IT SEEMS YOU HAVE BEEN VERY NEGATIVE
AND YOUR CHOICES IN LIFE, NOT VERY SELECTIVE
YOU HAVE BEEN USING AND DOING THINGS THAT
ONLY PLEASES YOU
AND IT SEEMS THAT THEY HAVE BEEN HARMFUL TOO
BUT YOU THOUGHT AS LONG AS YOU COULD GET BY
YOU NEED NOT ASK THE QUESTION, WHY
WELL, YOU HAD TO KNOW THE DAY WOULD SOON
COME ALONG
WHEN YOU WOULD QUESTION, WHERE DID I GO
WRONG
THAT DAY HAS COME, YOUR TIME IS NEAR
AND THAT IS WHY YOU FOUND ME HERE
THEN, WITH ONE STROKE OF HIS POWERFUL HAND
HE CHANGED MY OUTLOOK, SAYING, NOW YOU
UNDERSTAND
THERE ARE NO SHORTCUTS, THEY END UP COSTING
YOU MORE
TODAY IS FREE, TODAY YOU FOUND WHAT YOU WERE
LOOKING FOR
JUST REMEMBER, MY WORKS ARE REAL, MY PROMISES
TRUE
NOW GO SPREAD THE WORD OF WHAT I HAVE DONE
FOR YOU

DO NOT USE MY WORDS SPARINGLY, FOR I TELL YOU
TRUE
JUST A LITTLE "GAB" WILL NOT DO YOU

WRITTEN BECAUSE OF WHAT BROTHER MITCH
PREACHED ON ONE NIGHT, CALLED,
JUST A LITTLE DAB WILL DO YOU . . . I TOOK IT TO
MEAN THAT SOME PEOPLE THINK THAT PRAYING
SOMETIMES, OR GOING TO CHURCH A FEW TIMES, WAS
ALL THEY NEED TO SAY THEY WERE A CHRISTAIN . . . .

Keri/Raven/Corey

To my children, I have watched the year play out
I still see you all in mourning, so much in doubt
I wanted the best for all of you
I only wish there was more I could do
But, staying in mourning will not help
Do not rely on others you must do for your self
You are a part of me, my generation to carry on
My two daughters and my son
A grandchild has now been added to our family
Making us now, generation number, three
So, I ask you all to please take care of each other
Live your life for God, so one day, we will all again be together

Written for Ker1, Raven, Corey upon the one year remembrance of their Father, Earl Miles who passed away/ Dec. 2012

+KYLA

As I hold your hand and look at you today
Please know it is from my heart, these words to you, I say
God brought us together, and for fourteen years
We have found much happiness, and weathered many tears
But, as our years together keeps getting longer and longer
Our love for each other, also just gets stronger and stronger
The day we first met, you became the APPLE of MY EYE
For you stirred within me, a love I could not deny
Without you Kyla, I am nothing, being with you makes me feel whole
That is why I love you Kyla, with all my heart and soul
Today, before family, friends and the good Lord above
I vow again to you, my eternal love

Laying Down My Pen

I think that this is the last book of poems I will write
But, before I lay down my pen, I would, if I might
Say to everyone, yes, each and all
The wonderful people I met, you were the answer to my call
We shared together our heartaches, pain and happiness too
I would not be where I am if it were not for you
Your confidence in what I could do meant so much
I pray that somehow we all still try and stay in touch
But just remember, you do not have to be a poet or a writer
To write words that are comforting, or makes your heart feel lighter
All it takes is a little time and your DEVOTION
To put into words, your feelings of EMOTION

It is to all of you that I dedicate my book . . . there are so many that
I cannot name them all, because that would fill a book by itself, you
all know who you are and I thank you so very much . . . there are a
few I would like to name and I want them to know that I love them
so much for standing by me, especially during those difficult times I
had, for encouraging me when I began writing, having faith in me
MY FAMILY
My husband Royce, my childen, Michael, Mark{who has passed},
Steven and daughter Mellisa . . . my beautiful grandchildren, nine
of them, Crystle, Keri, Johnny, Brittany, Ashley, Royce, Tressa, Tori,
Steven, Jr., I am also blessed with six great grandchildren, Brianna,
Blake, Braylon, Kyle Jr., Alonica, Kahliena
Yes, I feel so blest to have so many blessings, not only the friends,
my church family you are all my family, and my own wonderful,
wonderful family, of which God made me a part of, but, the one
Blessing, the one without whom I would not be here or have come
this far for He gave me the words and the spiritual guidance . . .
thank you for choosing me to be a part of Your Family
JESUS CHRIST . . . my LORD and SAVIOUR

<u>LEONA</u>

Leona knew when she and Sammy became husband and wife
That God had Blest them and they would be "Soul Mates" for life
Together they became stronger, as daily their Faith increased
In their love for each other and God, a love that never ceased
Yes, struggles they had, but they always kept their Faith
For with it and God, they knew they would always be safe
And so it was when Leona became so ill
She never lost her Faith, and she kept a strong will
Even when the Doctor gave her a time, she said, "NO"
Only God knew when it would be time for her to go
She shared with all another birthday, her God given day
Before God whispered to her, you are ready, I am on My way
Leona never felt her burden was something she could not bear
She knew this was something that she and her God would share
When I first heard of her passing, I will not deny
My heart broke, I knelt, I prayed and I cried
For Leona was not only a friend to me
She was a friend to all, and she always tried to be
The walking example of what God wants from all of us
To love one another, and in God, put our trust
Leona, you made an impact on all of us
And we will miss you so very, very much
But in memory and Spirit with us you will always remain
Till we meet again, in HEAVEN'S GREAT DOMAIN

<u>LEONA GREEN THOMPSON</u>
9-27-1954------10-04-2013

LEST WE FORGET

Someone is forgetting that this is a country of choice
And everyone in it has a voice
But suddenly, we are being told what to wear
If we get sick, we have to have Obama Care
Well if we get sick, surely we would all know
Who our Dr. is and where we should go
We have welcomed here everyone, from all around
Even the Illegals who have come on America's ground
We elected officials who were to take care of us
But, somehow when they got to Washington, they lost touch
We are now being told in what or who to believe
They are letting them take away our place to worship or grieve
Banning our Christmas Holidays and caroling, an American tradition
Closing our shelters and even our missions
Saluting our Flag has become a NO-NO
Respect for our Veterans has hit a new low
Now they are choosing the foods that we eat
No more chocolates, candy, cookies or anything sweet
Taking away foods we want, they say it is making us fat
Now what kind of government is that?
If we want something, we need permission, now let me understand
We do not know what is good for us, so, Big Brother has to hold our
hand

Well, I am not a child and my body belongs to me
I do not want Big Brother, my Government telling me what I need
If I no longer can eat, think, live my life, then, I am no longer free
I might as well be dead, but, it was not the sweets and fats that killed
me

And the cruelty of mankind has reached its peak
There can be no more peace and then, only death will we seek
So, when I die, do an autopsy on me
And the cause was will be found to be
Due to lack of freedom, the heart gave up, it finally ceased
For only in death, would I find peace and be me

LETTING GOD IN

This morning I awoke with great anticipation
I was waiting to get out of my bed
I was no longer afraid of what temptation
I would find before me on the road ahead

Somehow I just knew that on the darkest day
The Sun would surely, brightly shine
I knew I only needed to let God lead the way
For I trusted Him and He was more than a friend of mine

God never left me He was always by my side
He always found a way to fill my empty heart
And this day I knew my prayer to Him would not be denied
As I cried out to Him, "oh God, how great Thou art"

Today God sent me down this path
That would change the rest of my life
God sent a friend that would again make me laugh
Help me as I struggled through my pain and strife

God, I give thanks and praise to You every day
For all your love and for filling my empty heart
I now know if we do not let God in or open that door
Then we will never find the peace and love that we are searching for

Looking at Your Picture Today

I held your picture and all I could see
Was this handsome young man looking back at me
No words were needed to be spoken that day
For we knew in our hearts what each one wanted to say
Silence is Golden, so I have heard
Your picture said it all, it was worth a thousand words

**MEMORIES OF MY SON MARK AS I HELD HIS PICTURE
TODAY
CLOSE TO MY HEART**

Looking for the Door

Did you ever keep trying to open a door
Hoping on the other side, you find what you are looking for?
But, once it was opened, to your surprise
You discovered it had always been there before your very eyes
It is just that sometimes we take things for granted
Letting our views of things to sometimes become slanted
Judgement calls on others then we tend to make
Forgetting that we too have made mistakes
We are never satisfied we keep wanting more and more
We keep trying to find what is behind that other door
Once we find that door and we go inside
We find those things that to us have never been denied
God said that your heart is that door
That had to be opened before you find what you are looking for
God said that the key to open that door
Was a forgiving heart, that you are looking for
Forgiveness must come from the heart, from within
Without forgiveness, God says in Heaven you cannot enter in

Love Cannot Be One Way

If I give to you my love and tell you that I care
It will be a love that only you and I should share
My love is not based on what I can get
But of lasting memories I never want to forget
I prayed that I would find someone like you
God answered my prayer and today we said "I do"
It is a commitment we have made to each other
Not to be broken and shared by a friend, a sister or a brother
For me, I can only love one at a time
And I will love you as long as you are only mine
There will be no forgiveness if I ever lose your trust
Or accepting your excuse, it was not love it was only lust
For when you let the flesh become a form of desire
Then it tends to make you a cheat and a liar
Adam and Eve were happy til the Serpent crawled in
Convincing them the naked body was a temptation for some to stray
But God never wanted our bodies used in that way
God never wanted the flesh to be used for temptation and pleasure
But for the bonding of love and creating new life
Joining together as one, husband and wife

LOVE IS

Love is a word that is so freely used
Love is a word that we sometimes abuse
Love is so freely spoken, thrown around
Love is a word that can make you feel good or let you down
Love, in so many languages it is spoken
Love can create a marriage, or cause one to be broken
Love should be sincere when shown or given to a friend
Love should be unconditional, it should never end
Love means different things to all of us
Love means affection, friendship, and trust
Love can sometimes seem like it is controlling
Love can make some feel like they have to be, beholding
Love is a word we all long to hear
Love should come from the heart, it must be sincere

LOVE . . . MOST WANTED and NEEDED
IT'S FREE

No flowers, no jewelry, none of that stuff
That some think in giving, is thanks enough
I can even buy you a new outfit, yes I can do that
Even add to the outfit, a new pocketbook, shoes and a hat
Or, I could send you on a well deserved trip
Maybe even a cruise, across the ocean on a ship
Take you to a movie, {you may have already seen}
Take you out dancing now that would be keen
All these things to some will sound great, and in good taste
But, Mother, knowing you, you will say, "it's a waste"
I would rather you come by for a visit, a cup of coffee or tea
Finding time to just spend with me
I just want a hug, a kiss and for you to stay in touch
To tell me you love me, that's not asking too much
No Mother, it's not, put the coffee pot on, I'm on my way
To spend time with you this Mother's Day

Mary Ann
God Said Your Book Was Full

Jesus said He died on the cross for you and me
To show how much He loved us, wanting us to believe
So, when Mary Ann entered that day through Heaven's Door
God said, your work is now finished, there was no more
You served me well while on this earth
You have followed me faithfully from the day of your birth
The family you raised was your pride and your joy
They filled you with love, only once you felt a void
When a child you loved was taken away
A part of you also left that day
But you taught your children never to waiver
From their teaching to love their Savior
Yes my child, your book is well filled
Because God said you obeyed Him and did His will
Because of your compassion for the sick and your fellow man
You went into nursing, saying, "I need to do all that I can"
Your smile to them every day was like a ray of sun light
Giving the sick encouragement, gave them the will to fight
But then soon, you too fell ill, even losing your sight
But you never complained, saying, God was your light
You were a devoted wife, a loving Mother
And you never stopped with your devotion to others
Mary Ann, the word THANK YOU, you heard many times
You would just smile, say, "you're welcome, the pleasure was all
mine"

Words cannot express how we all feel
Words cannot describe your smile or its' appeal
Words will not bring you back, I know
But the words now written in your memory will show
Just how much you will be missed and how we loved you so
You were a lady with so much love
You were indeed, an Angel, God sent to us from above
When your work here was completed
God took you home, where you beside Him you now will be seated
Your body again is whole, all your pain has now ceased
You are Home Mother, we love you, rest in peace

TO THE FAMILY OF MY CLASSMATE AND FRIEND
MARY ANN MANN FARRELL

MARY ANN

I got a call today, and the first words I would hear
Were, "I am sorry, we have just lost a loved one so dear"
They said she had passed quietly today
That she was at peace when God took her away
Her family has now all gathered round
Sharing with each other, memories in photos they have found
She lived a good life while here on earth
So proud of her family and children God gave her to birth
Though the loss of her parents, sister, and child brought much sorrow
She never gave up, she knew there would always be a tomorrow
Mary Ann then entered into the Medical field
Helping others as long as she could before she too became ill
Although she struggled with her own pain
She never gave up and she never complained
Always an inspiration to us all
Telling us that God was there to pick us up if we should fall
She said we should pray and keep the Faith
Not to rush God because His testing is part of the wait
Mary Ann as a classmate and a friend you stood out and apart
From all the others and you won everyone's heart
After graduation we all went our separate way
Staying in touch and hoping to see each other again one day
I thank God for the times that we all met
They are memories that I will never forget
Mary Ann, we will all miss you so very much
But, we will never forget you, your love and your special touch
I know that the Heaven's Gates have opened wide
And the Angels are singing, we've been waiting, please come inside
MARY ANN FARRELL

**WRITTEN FOR A WONDERFUL CLASSMATE AND
FRIEND WHO PASSED AWAY TODAY, Feb. 09th, 2014**

MAGIN

I am in a place where I am now free
And all my loved ones, I can still see
I have been in transit, because I too
Could not accept what had happened to me, just like all of you
It all happened so quickly that mournful day
When God reached down and took me away
No time to say good-bye, it came as a shock
Now these memories, so many have tried hard to block
Yes, that day changed so many lives, but you must still go on
You cannot change or undo what has been done
But, I ask you, do not blame God for calling me home
Do not keep crying and feel like you were the only one left alone
My grandchildren, your children, who seen me lying there that night
Needs your love, and comfort, assuring them, everything will be
alright
I asked God, "why me"?, and now I know why God brought me here
It was so I could watch over the ones I held so dear
When you had your accident, God sent me down to be by your side
And I watched over you, and I held your MOTHER as she cried
God told me it was not your time, you had children who still needed
you
To help them grow, and to be a part of their lives too
Magin, you must stay strong for them, stay in PRAYER
Know that wherever you go, I too will always be there
I know you that you are hurting, and I do understand
But, I also know that your future is in God's HAND
I want you to know that I will watch over you from above
Take this time God has given to you, to live, be happy and to love

MAGIN

I know why you mourn me, and I see why you weep
It is because of your love for me, and a heartache that is so deep
God blessed me with you and other loved ones that held me so dear
But, I want you to know I am at peace, I am at a better place here
I will always be there with you, I will always be nearby
So please do not keep mourning for me, or forever cry
For when remembering my passing, your sorrow bears down on
your heart
Do not think of my leaving as your life ending, but as my new start
I now know that there was nothing on earth, I now can see
My love for you does not compare to the love of God has for you
and me
You must now reach out to God for the answers you seek
With Him you can overcome any challenge you will meet
I am still with you in your heart and soul
I am with you always, wherever you go

**MAGiN, YOUR FATHER SEES YOUR PAIN, YOUR HURT, YOUR NOT UNDERSTANDING OF WHY ALL THIS HAPPENED AND HOW IT HAPPENED, BUT, THOUGH IT WAS NOT HIS CHOICE TO LEAVE SO QUICKLY WITHOUT SAYING GOODBYE, HE HAS AND IS STILL MOVING ON AND HE WANTS YOU TO DO THE SAME, FOR UNTIL YOU COME TO ACCEPT THE REALITY THAT HE IS NO LONGER HERE, HE TOO CANNOT MOVE ON . . . THERE MUST BE PEACE ON HEART ON BOTH SIDES, HIS TO MOVE INTO THE NEXT LEVEL, YOURS TO MOVE ON WITH YOUR LIFE, YOUR HUSBAND AND CHILDREN . . . THEN, AND ONLY THEN WILL YOU HAVE PEACE . . . YOU CAN NO LONGER LIVE IN A DREAM WORLD, YOU MUST LIVE IN THE HERE AND NOW, REALITY, THE REALITY IS THAT HE IS GONE, HE LOVED YOU, AND HE WILL ALWAYS BE WITH YOU, IN SPIRIT AND MEMORY
GOD BLESS YOU AND YOUR FAMILY, MEGAN**

MEMORIAL DAY WEEKEND
May 18, 2013

TODAY WE GIVE HONOR AND SALUTE TO ALL OF
THOSE
MEN AND WOMEN, WHOSE SERVICE TO THEIR
COUNTRY THEY CHOSE
THEY GAVE FREELY OF THEIR LIVES
SO OUR COUNTRY AND OUR FREEDOM WOULD
FOREVER SURVIVE
SADLY, REWARDS THEY HAVE GOT HERE ARE VERY FEW
BUT, GOD SAID, "A REWARD IN HEAVEN IS AWAITING
ALL OF YOU"
A SIMPLE THANK YOU, A SHAKE OF THE HAND
SAYING, I WANT TO HELP YOU TOO, IF I CAN
GOD BLESS AND THANK YOU, IS ALL WE CAN SAY
AS WE REMEMBER AND SALUTE YOU, THIS MEMORIAL
DAY

MEMORIES
MR. LEE PIERCE
JAN. 11th, 2010

Loved ones and friends have gathered here
To say good-bye to a loved one so dear
A beloved brother, father and friend
He was someone on whom you could always depend
He was gentle, peaceful, quiet, he was one of a kind
Stayed by himself, to his own business he tried to mind
But he was always there to give and to share
This wonderful man, a man who truly did care
He believed in truth and honesty from all of us
But for those who lied to him, he held in disgust
Reputation was very important to him, whether yours or his own
And he believed in fighting for truth, saying it had to be known
Yes, this was truly a man you could or would not forget
And in our hearts, his memory is forever etched
Mr. Lee, I knew you for such a very short time
But on me, a lasting impression and memory you left behind
My grandson Steven put you right up there on top
Of men he looked up to, just like his own "POP"
Mr. Lee, life for all of us will now have a void without you
For you truly left your mark on all those you met and knew
Your sister Pat, she was always there by you side
She was also a great friend whose love could never be denied
Be proud of the memories that you have left
Memories not forgotten, even in death
GOD saw your pain and He came down to say
"It is time, I have come for you today"
Mr. Lee, your body is now whole, your pain has now ceased
GOD BLESS YOU MR. LEE, MAY YOU REST IN PEACE

MERRY CHRISTMAS
December 22, 2013

This Holiday Season, we will gather and remennince
Sharing memories and remembering loved ones so dearly missed
We will all gather around the Christmas tree
Each of us speaking of so many happy memories
But, let us not dwell on memories that are sad
But, let us be thankful for things we still have and once had
Be thankful, for we still have something far better than wealth
We are rich because we have family, friends, and our health
Though many of our loved ones have now passed
They left with us, memories that will forever last
Be thankful and happy when celebrating this Christmas morn
Remember, it is the day that Jesus Christ, our Savior was born
So today, with my family and friends, so many memories I too will recall
Today another happy memory I will add, MERRY CHRISTMAS to you all
+++
+++++++++++++
Pastor Kenny
KGM
Pastor Kenny, this is your first Christmas celebrating in your new church and I just wanted to let you know that I love you all and you are all forever etched in my mind, my heart . . . For some, this day I know will bring memories of loved ones that have passed, but, God lets us all deal with our pain and loss in our own way, and He is there with us all to give us comfort
PASTOR KENNY/ BONITA & ANGIE
There are too many to say all your names, but, to all of you I remember you, I thank you all for your friendship over the years, know that you all truly made an impact on me and changed my life in so many ways

I have written several books with so many of my friends and people I have known in them, but, the most important book is the one God has written and I pray I and all my family and friends are in the final chapter of HIS BOOK of ETERNAL LIFE
<u>GOD BLESS & HAVE A BLESSED DAY</u>

Misunderstood
Choosing my Words

Why do people say, "I'm not sure of what I just said
Whatever it was, I think into the words, people just misread"
Yes, I was angry and the words that I wrote
Certainly did not get me a popularity vote
So to those who knew the words were meant just for you
I say I am sorry for posting it for all to view
It is all over and done and if I ever do it again
I promise to call you first before I post and send
So to all the others who would take this route
Be careful what you say, let your words leave no doubt
Sometimes words that are supposed to be a compliment
Can be misunderstood, not what you meant
Choose them wisely, think them through
You will get more respect from others when you do

MOTHER

Mother, I see all your family making a fuss over you
Not just because of who you are, but for all you do
All our grandchildren and loved ones I see giving you a kiss
Saying "we love you, you are number one on our list"
You will get so emotional, I know you will
When they all show you and tell you how they feel
But, you deserve it Mother, for you are the best
To me, you stand apart, from all the rest
Mother, I want you to feel my presence with you today
If you listen closely you will also hear me say
Mother, I love you with all my heart
We will never be separated or apart
The Lord in His wisdom gave to me
A Mother who gave me happiness and so much glee
So, on this day, from my home in Heaven above
I send to you, a very special love
HAPPY MOTHER'S DAY

**WRITTEN FOR BETTY EVANS
HER FIRST MOTHER'S DAY AFTER THE PASSING OF HER
SON
KEVIN EVANS**

MR. PRESIDENT . . . WHY?

Mr. President, I have to ask the question, 'why'?
Why have you chosen our children's rights to deny?
You have taken away their tour of the White House, a Historical Site
By doing so, you have taken away a much fought for and anticipated right
Even we the people look forward to the yearly White House Tour
It is a freedom, a promise that we have lost, temporarily, that's for sure
In the meantime, you have two children living there, they have lost nothing
But, Mr. President, you have left our children, sad and no longer trusting
They are special, these chosen few who travels and sees so much more
But, our children cannot even get into the WHITE HOUSE door
They have lost the honor and respect of you, Mr. President
And they no longer have faith in their own Government
They feel that they are being pushed aside for a chosen few
Like rich families and movie stars, just to name one or two
Mr. President, the White House belongs to all of us
Not just for these with the Midas Touch
There has to be ways that our government can cut some costs
Without it hurting the people, or making them take a loss
We need to all begin to work together, united as one
No matter which side of the aisle they are own
For one day, their families too will be left to travel that road
But, if we're all separated, who will be left to help carry their load

Mr. President/What Happened?

MR. President, I have to ask, "What happened to you?"
You were given the chance to make a dream, be a reality come true
So many people who, in you believed and trusted
Have now become ashamed, and even disgusted
You got the chance to become the very first one
Of your race, to have the American Dream, and overcome
Martin Luther King fought for these dreams to come true
Giving you the chance to become an example, and a leader too
John F. Kennedy had to overcome bias, in the form of Religion
But, he overcame, the voters knew in him they had made the right
decision
They all knew it would be an uphill fight
But, they vowed to fight for the people and their rights
They did not try to force upon them their views
But, gave us the right to vote, use our voice, and to choose
Mr. President, the voters did not say to you, "he is black, let's give
him a turn"
You would not have been voted into office if there had been a racial
concern
The voters really felt a confidence in you, in you they placed their
trust
Because you promised us all, that you would be just
Yes, you promised us that you would seek
To end the wars in the Middle East, bringing us peace
You said that you would strive to end this racial hatred
Returning unity to the country, we all hold sacred
You promised us that there would be transparentcy
Another promise broken, for that one too, we have yet to see
Instead, you have created hate and hostility even more
Dividing us, bringing distrust between ourselves and our neighbors
next door

Our Allies are growing more and more uneasy with us
Our enemies think we are weak and an easy touch
You act like only you have the answer, you know what's best
Then you try to force your views on all the rest
I was told George Washington was the Father of our country
As President, he led us to freedom and gave us liberty
Mr. President, you could have become the man of the hour
But, you became consumed with too much power
I now believe you will go down in history
As the President, shrouded in so much mystery
But, as always, if you are looking for someone to blame
Blame the voters who voted for you . . . to them I say, SHAME . . .
SHAME . . . SHAME

My Brother Ray

Ray, it was hard for me to let my feelings come through
I was never able to say the things I wish I had said to you
I hope you knew my feelings and how proud I was to be
Your brother and that we were family
Although our lives went into different directions
We never lost the respect for each other and our affection
You were always there for me, coming back into my life
To help me out when I had so much strife
You gave to me and also to my sons
Jobs most needed when we had no income
You seemed always to be able to find
Work for all of us, no matter what kind
You became part of my son's church, he would now start
You and your family came, supporting him with all your heart
I know what you did to give it financial support
No one needed to show me the monthly report
Later in years, time together we finally began to share
Going fishing, taking trips, anytime and anywhere
Ray, you were always there for me
I felt we were as close as any two brothers could be
During my illness, you never left my side
You tried to be strong, but, your emotions you could not hide
I always felt your presence and it gave me such peace
I want you to know that I am now free and my pain has ceased
I feel comfort knowing you and Shirley will always be there
To help my Angie, giving her comfort and showing you care
Yes, I know you will take care of her, but, give her some space
Just keep her busy, she takes her time, does nothing in haste
Ray, because you are faithful to God, you believe in His Power
A loving family and Blessings upon you God has showered

You have thanked God by helping out your fellow man
And God has prepared for you a home in the Promised Land
God has promised we will be together again some day
I am so proud to call you my brother RAY

**I WROTE THESE WORDS I FELT BRO. J.C. GRIFFIN
WANTED TO SAY TO HIS
BROTHER, RAY, WHO WAS NOT JUST HIS BROTHER,
BUT, HIS CONFIDENT, HIS FRIEND,
SOMEONE THAT HE COULD TALK TO AND DEPEND
UPON
HENRY {RAY} GRIFFIN**

MY CHILD

Lynette, I see your heart, you are feeling so alone
You feel lost, there is no place you can call home
My child, I heard your prayers and I heard your cry
But you must believe, it is who you must try
For I have sent down Angels as you asked me too
But you pushed them aside, wanting them to stay away from you
The Devil has put you in His chains
Hoping to bring you down into His hell of flames
Now, only you can take control
Over who is going to take your soul
You can stand up straight, hold your head up high
Tell Satan leave me, for my Savior I will no longer deny
Yes, he will hang around just to make sure
But will leave quickly when he sees your heart is again pure
I am here with you always, you will never be alone
And one day you can call Heaven your home

MY CLASSMATES OF "55"

When I look back at this memorable year in time
So many of my classmates that year come to mind
Though some of them have gone on and it saddened us
They too are remembered, they are missed so very much
Our reunions are fantastic, when so many of us gather here
To go over and catch up on memories we hold so dear
To all the young men who were in my class
I think of all of you as, a "first class act"
To the young ladies of my class, just a word or two
I thank you for just being you
Barbara, Alice, Donna, Diane
Dixie, Gertrude, Hazel, Mary Anne
Betty, Inez, and not forgetting Alice number #2
Words cannot express how much I appreciate all of you
Not only were we classmates, but we were friends who bonded
together
And through the years we managed to stay in touch with each other

Though I do not get to see you all very much
We still write or call, but somehow, we keep in touch
God gave me words, I wrote some of them for you
About your loved ones passing, which were my classmates too
You all soon became a part and a reason for this book of mine
I will never forget you, you all will always be in my heart and on my
mind

My Country/My Government
What Happened?

Yes, this is my country, my country of freedom, we love and praise
So why do we need to fight within our borders, our country to save?
Is it because our voices and our freedom are slowly being lost?
The freedom that our forefathers fought for, at a cost
Our government is taking Prayer out of our school
No more teaching our children to obey the Golden Rule
They are trying to take away our rights to pick and choose
Even to our voices, they are trying to silence and make us lose
Our government says, "we will now take care of you
If you will just bow down and quietly do
What we, the government thinks is right
Even though it may not be to your approval or delight"
Our system is caught up in so much cheating
That even our jobs and income have taken a terrible beating
Our countries financial system has hit an all time high
While our unemployment has gone through the roof, to the sky
But, our government just shrugs and says, "what's all the fuss?
We will help you out we will give you a stimulus
A stimulus for who?, it is not for you or me
But for big Corporations and selected Companies
You ask our young men to go to war
But, they now are asking, "what are we fighting for?"
Our government does not want us to honor our dead
Or help our Veterans who have fought for our country and bled
You are making us take down the crosses, where ever they are
Because a minority says it represents religion, they want it barred
Then, even to bring us down to greater shame
In some places we can no longer pray or say a Holy name
Who are these elected that have chosen to change the rule?

We elected you to fight for the majority, not just a chosen few
Yes, our government and laws do have some flaws
But, only because you keep trying to make/change the laws
We want our government to know that we will not run
That we, the majority will again be heard, WE WILL OVERCOME

My Friend . . . Polly McLeod

My heart skipped that day when
I first met Polly, who would forever become my friend
My feelings and fears with her I soon shared
Because I knew she really cared
She was an unexpected friend, who yes indeed
Reached out to me in my time of need
She took me in also as part of her family
Saying," God says we are like sisters, you and me"
But Polly is not only a friend to just me
She is always there for anyone in need
She will visit them in the hospital, or in their home
Bringing the word of God, assuring them they are not alone
I wish that we could see each other much more
Be nice if we lived close, like maybe next door
But we still call, keeping in touch
I enjoy this time with a friend that I have come to love so much
Polly, I want you to know that you are the reason
I began enjoying life, no longer thinking of leaving
God, I know sometimes when I pray
I fail to say thank you for sending Ms. Polly my way
So, before God and all I want to say I am so proud
To be a part of her life and have a friend like Polly Mcleod

**I TRULY BELIEVE THAT GOD SENDS PEOPLE INTO OUR
LIVES WHEN WE NEED SOMEONE
AND GOD BROUGHT POLLY INTO MY LIFE THROUGH
ANOTHER FRIEND, HER SISTER-IN-LAW
SHIRLEY McLEOD WHO HAS GONE ON TO BE WITH
HER HEAVENLY FATHER**

My Mother

She was a beautiful lady, with a lovely smile
She was there for us, always walking that extra mile
She always listened to our concerns and little whines
But reminded us that some things could only be learned in time
She told us to always try and do our very best
To put our trust in God and He would do the rest
For in this world in which we now live
We must learn to let go, forget and forgive
Her teachings and her love she gave to us all
To both family and friend, if needed, she said, "just give me a call"
Though she has gone, yes, but not even death
Could take away the teachings and memories that she has left
I still feel her presence, her warmth and loving touch
She was my Mother that I loved so very much

**WRITTEN FOR LISA ON THE ANNIVERSARY OF HER
MOTHER'S DEATH
GOD BLESS**

My Opinion

Just who do you think you are?
Someone they once called a "movie star"
What makes you think you are special and you are the one?
Who can tell our Leaders how they should run
Our country and our Foreign Affairs
Well, you need to ask someone you think cares
I am an American citizen, and here in the U.S.A.
Where I live in freedom, every day
I voted for our Leaders and trusted that they
Would keep us safe, in a peaceful way
I do not want to interfere
Every time there is a rumor that I hear
He may not have been your choice for now
But, that does not mean that you can tell him how
He should deal with our enemies when they dare
No matter who they are or where
Well, your opinion leaves lots of doubt
That is why our elected is in and you are out
Everyone has an opinion from time to time
And everyone has a right to speak their mind
But, if you consort with our enemies from afar
My opinion, you are no better than they are
But, you could not voice your opinion so openly
If you live in enemy country, for you would not be free
My country, America is free; I want to keep it that way
And for peace, I will continue every day to Pray
Speaking against our leaders in enemy countries is wrong
If you do, then maybe that is where you belong
Luckily, yours is just an opinion, our leaders make our decisions
And I believe they will do it with the utmost precision

My Reasons for Living

God has been so good to me
One daughter I had, sons, I had three
I was so proud of them, watching them grow
I loved them all equally, I pray this they know
Mellisa/Michael/Steven and my son Mark
He left us all early, but he remains forever in our heart
They grew up, had their own families
Gave me grandchildren, gosh, I was so pleased
Nine all total, six girls and three boys
Each one a delight, bringing so much joy
Johnny, Royce, Steven, this old heart they truly won
Three loving, caring, wonderful grandsons
Crystle, Keri, Brittany, Ashley, Tressa and Tori
Beautiful, caring, loving, and liberated, now that's another story
The years pass so quickly, now, they are all grown
Some became married, now have children of their own
Yes, six great-grandchildren, I now have, what a Blessing
But still more to come, I sure am hopin', not just guessin'
Brianna/Blake/Alonica/Kahlena/Braylon and Brandon {K.J.}
You are all God's Blessings He has sent my way
Thank you God for all these wonderful blessings you sent to me
Thank you God for such a wonderful family

MY VOTE

This little vote of mine
I want to make it count
This little vote of mine
I want to make it count
Make it count, make it count, make it count

Let those machines throw them out, NO
I want my vote to count
Let those machines throw them out, NO
I want my vote to count
Make it count, make it count, make it count

Hide it under a Bush-el NO
I want to make it count
Hide it under a Bush-el NO
I want to make it count
Make it count, make it count, make it count

Count it all over, if you must
I only what is fair and just
Count it all over, if you must
I only want what is fair and just
So, count my vote, count my vote, count my vote

**Written about the voter problems in Fla, in Nov., 2001
Sung to the tune of, THIS LITTLE LIGHT of MINE**

Nobody Asked Me

Nobody asked me if I would run
Boy, oh boy, could I have fun
I am a natural at organizing
You should see my family, I am still downsizing
I do my own laundry, my own shopping too
Make appointments with Doctors and Teachers, just to name a few
I balance my own checkbook, I dare not overdraw
Because making a mistake could be costly to all
I listen to confessions, hear many lies
Hearing blame put on others and switching sides
Then, I would make a decision on who to believe
But, I had to decide what the outcome would be
So why do I think that I am qualified?
Just keep listening and I think you will be satisfied
I am a homemaker, I have a family too
So, it is only common sense that a Mother would know what to do
I have been a wife, a friend, a Mother, just to name a few
A teacher, a counselor, and yes, an auditor too
A chauffeur, a maid, a chef, and a dietician
Even sometimes a practicing Physician
Did housework, yard work and that's not all
I was always on, 24 hour call
I did not need a limo to take me somewhere
I did it all, because I cared
The monies being spent and thrown around
Just because some want to bring each other down
I could put all that money in one big sack
I would have enough money to bring the debt, from Red to Black
And I will not make a promise that I cannot keep
But, on my watch, you will not catch me asleep

Written when everyone was trying to run for Governor of California {recall}

Only God can Heal

When the heart finally becomes still
That is the time our heartaches and pain will heal
Yes, pain from the loss of loved ones we will always feel
But we now know life goes on, we must go forward, begin to deal
With each new day now, because life does not stand still
We must deal with what is now past and what is real
For though we have said our final good-byes
Their memories are with us forever, our love for them never dies
We must learn to put our faith in God, for only He can heal
With God, we will overcome, and yes, we will learn to deal

ORDINATION

Last night I sat and I began to read
From my Bible, words that I surely did need
I wanted them to be just right
If I were going to speak them tonight
We are all chosen by God, this is true
But God's faithful servants are becoming far too few
For when God's chosen accepts God with all his heart
Then all earthly things from him must now depart
He must walk that narrow path, follow the road
That Jesus went down, when He too carried our heavy load
We know that road will lead us to the foot of the Cross
And we must also walk that road or we will be lost
So tonight we will gather to welcome the man
Who gave his commitment to God, saying, "I will and I can"
He promised to serve God in whatever He asks
That he would be ready, whatever the task
There is now joy in Heaven, because on this day
Another one of God's chosen was heard to say
That he would commit to God, to sing and to give Him praise,
To do all His works, in God's ways
To counsel, to Pray, to spread His word
To all in need and wherever it could be heard
He promised to shed from his earthly body all his sins
For today he was reborn and a new life he would see begin
Jack asked God to give him the wisdom that he will need
To now go out and begin to plant God's seed
Pastor Kenny and Lakeside Outreach Ministries want to say,
God Bless you Jack Barkley, on this new road you chose today

**Written for Jack Barkley upon his acceptance of being Ordained by
Pastor Kenneth Griffin**

OUR ENVIROMENT

Help me, help me, I want to breathe
I used to it with such an ease
I once could see the Sun each early morn
See the beauty of the life around it was so adorned
I used to see the Moon as it beheld the night
In all of its beauty, Heaven's eternal light
I watched the animals drink from the waters so pure
But, the place they drink are getting fewer and fewer
My friends, we did this disaster, the terrible deed
Because of our own selfishness and our greed
Yes, we have polluted our precious air
By ignoring it and acting as though we did not care
My friends, we need to wake up while we can
Lifting our voices and taking a stand
If we do not take a stand, then it's good-bye Earth
For there will be no more vegetation, life or rebirth
Yes, everything is reaching out for air
And friends, we are still acting like we do not care
It is because of us that everything is soon dying
A fact that we all seem to just keep denying
One day very soon, for it will not be too long
It will be too late we will wake up to find everything gone
The woods will no longer be green
The beautiful birds, they no longer will sing
Wildlife all gone, no animals running around
There will be complete silence, not a sound
Each generation must strive to find the solution
To stop the smog and all the pollution
For this, we all must strive
If another generation is to survive

OUR SISTER BEA

Today as we gather around our sister we loved so dear
We are remembering a sister who gave us so much happiness and
cheer
For as each of us were born, it seemed we were bonded together
To live our lives independently, but dependent upon each other
We also lived our lives for God who has been so good to us
Bringing into our lives friends who have come to mean so much
Friends who would often stop by just to talk while having coffee or
tea
And we looked forward to their visits and enjoyed their company
We always knew that God would one day call one of us to travel
ahead
And today, God has chosen the strongest, the one who always led
Today, we stand around her as God prepares to take her home
Letting her know memories she has left and we will never be alone
God promised us all that we would one day be together again
But, that only He would know the time or even when
So, Bea, we wait here together, waiting for God's will to be done
Doing God's will, till He calls us home, one by one
I know Heaven's Gates have opened wide so the Angels can receive
The next soul entering, our beloved sister, Bea
All your pain and suffering has now ceased
You are home, rest in Eternal Peace

Dedicated to the sisters of Bea McLeod
Varney, Ethel, Caroline, Vera{deceased}
Billy . . . her special soul mate

OUR VOICE

Did you ever take a moment and really pause
To think of your restrictions while trying to obey the new laws
Did you ever ask, "how did I get here, why am I on this earth?
Well, like all new things, it all begins with a new beginning called,
Birth
It is true that giving birth at one time we were all given a choice
Then, once we were born, God then gave to us a VOICE
So it is when a new law is birthed, before it is ready to enact
We the people have the right to read them and know the fact
We should not have to first pass a law
Before finding out its faults and its flaws
Then, having to fight to have them amended
Or maybe even having it completely recended
We should know what the new law means for me and you
For laws should be for all of us, not just a few
We are guaranteed freedom and equality under the law
Not for a minority or chosen few, but for all
To protect our freedom, we have fought for and won
We must have our voices heard and not be silenced by anyone
We are all here as one, whether it be by birth or by choice
We will all stand together, you will not drown out or silence our voice
So, let us continue to cry out, choosing what our future will be
Because it is our God given VOICE that will keep us free

OVIEDA ROSE
Feb. 06th, 1935-Jan. 19th, 2014
Time for the Season of the Soul has Come

Why am I so cast down and so despondently sad?
When all I long for is to be happy and glad
Why does my heart feel so heavy with so much weight?
All I want to do is escape from this soul-saddened state
I quietly ask God and myself why life has to be this way
Why has my happiness been silenced in a heart that was gay
But then God showed me and suddenly it all became so clear
That the Soul too has a Season just like the year
He said that I too must pass through life's Autumn of dying
Which is a desolate time of heartbreak, hurt, and crying
Then it is followed by Winter holding in it's frostbitten hand
My heart that has become as frozen as all the snow covered land
Yes, I now know I must pass through all the seasons that God sends
I am now content in knowing that one day everything ends
But what a Blessing it is to know that God has His reasons
And for us to find our Soul, we too must then have seasons
We get strength in knowing that the Autumn time sadness
Will soon be filled by a Springtime filled with gladness
Yes, God says that He chooses only the best
And today we see one of them being laid to rest
A wonderful, beautiful woman whom God has chose
Our loving Mother, Ovieda Rose

Feb. 06th, 1935-Jan. 19th, 2014

PATIENCE

They say patience is a virtue
But what is a person to do?
When you stand behind someone in line
Whose idle chatter is wasting my time.

They are not talking about anything
Just exercising their right to talk as a human being.
They ramble on, wagging their tongue
Gossiping about anything and anyone.

Well, I am tired of all this stuff
I have heard just about, quite enough.
So, if you do not want to hear my wrath
Then you better move, you are in my path.

Let me warn you about the 'short line'
People there just waste your time.
Go to the long aisle cause it moves fast
People there do not have time to hear about your past.

I was standing in an express line in a grocery store

Q.L./REMEMBERED
On Sept. 18th, one year ago on this day
A much beloved man was called away.
Though he left so quickly, no time to prepare
He left many memories, together his family will share.
We still are asking, "why did he have to leave"?
Yes, we miss him and together we will grieve.
He was a husband, a father, grandfather, and a friend
He was someone on whom we could all look to and depend.
Family reunions will for us still be, they are a must

Q. L. loved reunions, they had to have his final touch.

He loved to hear the songs, sung by Allen, his son

Especially, "you are my rock, you are the one I can depend on".

Though Q.L. knew the song was speaking of God

He liked to think that he too was part of that Rod,

For all the times, both good and bad, together, they all weathered

And it made them stronger, kept them all together.

Q.L. loved his wife Betty, and his fast growing family,

He is up there smiling, saying, "keep on spreading our family tree"

To my wife Betty, my family and all my loved ones I want to say

Just look toward Heaven, I did not leave you, I am not that far away.

WRITTEN FOR BETTY EVANS AND HER FAMILY
Q. L. EVANS

PRAYING-NO SET TIME

I used to set aside a time every day
When I would take the time to pray
I waited anxiously for that time to draw near
Vowing to let nothing or no one interfere
For it was that very special time
I could quietly sit with God and tell Him what was on my mind
But, one day when I began to pray
I heard a voice gently but quietly say,
"Why do you set just one special time aside for me,
For I am here with you always, whatever the need
Yes, I want you to have that quiet time
To spend with Me, telling me what is on your mind,
But the time you set aside should not always be
The only time that you talk to me
Prayers must be genuine and from the heart
From this I want you never to depart
Know that I am here, I am always around
Whenever you need Me, just call out, God, I need you now
If you need me, you know through prayer I can be found
You do not have to wait for Prayer Time to roll around"
To talk to me about whatever you need
Just take My hand, I will lead

Cashing in my Ticket

I'm taking a trip to the Promised Land
And my ticket is paid for, but not by man
But by my Jesus who died for me
Cleansed my Soul and set me free
God said, "you now have a way home
I will be with you, you will not be alone"
Your ticket is free, no money or material cost
Jesus already paid when He died upon the cross
I did His work while I was upon this land
Me and God walked together, hand in hand
I truly believed in Him
And tried to live my life, free of sin
God you promised me that when it was time
I would enter quickly, no standing in line
A ticket to Heaven you gave me when I was born
Said if I used it wisely, I could cash it in one morn
Lord I never exchanged that ticket or gave it away
For I knew it was my ticket to Heaven one day
Now, I am ready, I can hardly wait
To meet you at the Pearly Gate
When I hear those trumpets roll
I'll say, "pick me up Lord, I am ready to go"
God, I now know that I have passed all your tests
For I am boarding that Heavenly Express
The Angels have asked for my boarding pass
Thank God, Thank God, I am going home at last

RAINY DAY FRIENDS

I think it is cruel and not really fair
To tell someone you love them and that you care
But, when you are needed, you're never around
It seems like you just do not want to be found
I need a friend in whom I can confide
When I am going through a storm, they don't run and hide
For a friend is someone upon whom you depend
When you ask them for help, they readily say, "where and when?"
Rainy day friends will also one day need
A true friend, yes, they may even remember me
But, if I am your friend, and I tell you so
I do it from the heart, not just for show
So, if you tell a friend, you love them and you care
Tell them also, "if you need me, I will be there"

Raising Our Flag and Our Voices

Let us raise our Red-White-and Blue
Against all of those who are trying to
Take away our freedom in this, our own land
We need to lift our voices and take a stand
For over 200 years, many have died and fought
For freedom of Religion and schools where our children would be
taught
We cried out, this is our land, we all have freedom here
We can Pray, teach, and vote, making our voices heard without fear
There are many with dreams who are still coming from afar
Saying only in America, can we reach for the stars
We can worship freely, be whatever we choose to be
Sending our children to college, raising a family
Sadly, we are still fighting for things here have gone too far
Many of our voices, some in our Government has tried to bar
The laws are neglecting the majority, favoring a very few
More and more Americans are crying out, "what can we do?'
We can come together, raising our flag again and using our voice
To let our Government know, we elected you, we do have a choice
The perks and monies that you get to appease a few
Will soon be over, yes, our voices being quieted is long overdo
Because we will stand together, whether we are here by birth or by
choice
For this is our country, and freedom means that we all have a voice

RAVEN

Raven, I can still see you and I hear your cry
I can still hear your question, when you cry out "WHY"?
So many questions, I can see them in your heart
You're asking God why loved ones so quickly depart
God has a reason for each of us to be on earth
With you, I see God has blessed you, soon a child to birth
Yes, God says this child you will love and watch grow
And the answers to your questions, you will then know
For this is a responsibility only you can undertake
No time to feel sorry for yourself or make a mistake
When you do have a question, take it to Jesus, our Lord
And He will give you the answer that you are looking for
Raven, the Angels surround and keep you every day
And your father and I are near, we are not far away
We know you carry us daily in your heart
We will never be apart
You and your sister Keri are close, you are a team
You are both strong, remember, you have your father's genes

THIS WAS WRITTEN FOR RAVEN, WHO HAS HAD A
HARD TIME ADJUSTING TO OR UNDERSTANDING THE
PASSING OF HER BELOVED GRANDMOTHER CECILE
AND HER FATHER EARL . . . SHE IS NOW WITH CHILD
THAT WILL GIVE HER JOY, PEACE OF MIND, A REASON
TO BELIEVE AND TO GO ON WITH LIFE

REATHA

Here today lies a lady of such beauty, class and pride
Whose love and dedication to her family could never be denied
When it came to her family she let nothing interfere
Including her very promising Real Estate career
Her husband Gilford, she admired and loved him so
Left a deep void in her life when she had to let him go
But today she will again be with the man she so loved
Where they again will be together, forever in Heaven above
Her son Randy, she stood by him, had faith in what he would be
Like all good Mothers, she was right, so proud and happy was she
Her daughter Pam, they were so close, she gave her all the love God
allowed
So proud of her, saying she stood out anywhere, in any crowd
Three wonderful caring brothers she also had
Buford{Boo}/Royce{Roddy}/and Talmadge{Tad}
Yes, they all took care of their sister, that's a fact
You might say that they "scratched each others back"
A sister, Norma Nell, was the "baby" of the family and Reatha made
sure
That no matter what, she would always be there and take care of her
As Norma Nell grew older and went out on her own
They always stayed in touch, by mail or by telephone
To all the grands, greatgrands, nieces and nephews too
You all know just how much she loved and cared for all of you
Her favorite son-in-law Benji, now she really cared for him a lot
For she knew he was always there for her, whether she needed him
or not

Reatha knew she had lots of family, love, and God in her life
All comforting and important when she had sorrow or strife
The memories that Reatha has now left behind
Will be remembered forever, for she indeed was one of a kind
Her Mother, our GaGa, she will see as Heaven's Gates open wide
Where they will again walk together, side by side
Yes, today we say good-bye to a loving Mother, Grandmother, and
sister
She was much loved, will forever be remembered . . . we will all miss
her

March 17th .1926 . . . Oct. 6th . . . 2012
WRITTEN FOR HER CHILDREN, PAM FRANKLIN AND
RANDY PAIGE AND THEIR CHILDREN
HER BROTHERS AND SISTERS . . . BUFORD SCOTT/
TALMADGE SCOTT/ROYCE SCOTT/NORMA NELL SMITH
AND THEIR FAMILIES . . . . GOD BLESS

REV. LEO TIDWELL

I wanted to write a word or two
I wanted to make sure the right words I choose
For here was a man who was very respected
Because from his God and his Faith, he never defected
When God called upon him to spread his word
He went to the airwaves so he could really be heard
God blessed him with a family that he loved so
He would smile and thank God as he watched his family grow
24 Grand, 28 great grand and 01 great, great grand
Leo said they were his future, all part of God's plan
God called him home, but, you will still see
His legacy and his Tidwell Ministry
Because his beloved daughter and all the family will carry on
All the work that Rev. Tidwell had begun
We know that you have now gone to Heaven to make a place
For all of us, when we will again meet together, face to face
Today you heard the Angels ringing that Golden Bell
Saying, "welcome home", God's chosen, Rev. Leo Tidwell

**Written for the children and family of Rev. Tidwell . . . God's
blessings and comfort to each of you . . . . Rev. Tidwell . . . Rest
in Peace . . . your memories and work here will never cease**

REUNION
OUR FAMILY GATHERING

Well, here it is, another whole year
We give thanks to God, to all who could be here
Loved ones who have gathered from all around
Those who live close and those from out of town
Yes, this is our chosen time when we come together
Being able to hug and talk, not just by phone or by a letter
Time for catching up on all the news, both new and old
Listening to stories that our ancestors before us told
Our now older generation looking upon the young
Proud of how far, each generation has come
For now, each generation will carry on where the other left off
Carrying on a tradition that we hope will never stop
So, as we gather again this year, united as one
We will eat, enjoy being together, and have lots of fun
Then, God willing, we will meet again, same time next year
To again hold and embrace those that we hold so dear
God Bless and God speed, be safe returning to your home
Till we meet again, let's keep in touch by letter or by phone

**WRITTEN FOR MY SISTER IN CHRIST, MY FRIEND,
POLLY McLEOD FOR HER FAMILY REUNION
SATURDAY, MAY 4TH, 2013
THANK YOU POLLY FOR LETTING ME BE A PART**

ROBERT

Robert, my heart melted the day we first met
It is a day in my life that I will never forget
When I saw you, I knew then I would choose
The man I knew I never wanted to lose
I believe God brought us together because He knew
Just how much I needed someone like you
Standing there, you reminded me of a soft and cuddly TEDDY
BEAR
I just wanted to squeeze you, hold you, tell you how much I cared
Then, when you held me in your arms, you made me feel
Like a woman should and I knew that our love was real
We got married and though fourteen years have passed
Our love has bonded us to a marriage that will forever last
Our children of love also bonded us closer together
Making our lives special, like no other
We are sharing our happiness with friends and family today
As we stand before God, our vows, we again get to say
I love you Robert with all my heart, God only knows
How my love for you every day, just grows and grows
I love you Robert, my special TEDDY BEAR
It is forever with you, my love and life I want to share

**THIS WAS WRITTEN FOR A FRIEND
KYLA WATFORD
RENEWING OF HER WEDDING VOWS TO HER HUSBAND
ROBERT WATFORD**

ROBERT

Fourteen years ago when we first met
It became the beginning of my life, a day I will never forget
I fell in love with you then, I love you still
I always have and I always will
You gave to me a home, a family, someone to love
I know it was all because of a blessing from above
I call you my special TEDDY BEAR, this is true
Because they are so loveable and huggable, and so are you
Friends and family are to share with us today
As we stand before God, and again we get to say
Our vows of love to one another
To always be faithful and true to each other
So, as I place my hand in your hand again
Our love is renewed today, to heights we have never been
I love you Robert Watford
My wonderful, lovable
TEDDY BEAR

ROCK and ROLL MY SOUL

I have been told to jump and to shout
To let it all go, let it all hang out
To raise my voice in both song and praise
I am told, this is God's way

Well, if I do jump up and down, will I be closer to Him?
Or will He wonder if I am in church, or in a gym
And if I scream and shout, like a victory cheer
Will God say, "I'm not deaf, I can hear"?

Then, if I begin to wave my arms all around
Will He be up there, looking down
Saying, "I need no signals on how to land,
I only need to know just where you stand"

Well, when the Hold Ghost took hold of me
I felt an explosion you would not believe
I shouted and jumped and sang God's praise
My, what an exciting way to spend God's day

Yes, this old body did just what it was told
When the Holy Ghost entered and took hold
So, if you feel the ground beneath you begin to quake
It is me, beginning to jump, holler, shiver and shake

SHARING and REMEMBERING

BETTY, I said a Prayer for you today
ASKING God to send peace and comfort your way
I know it has been almost a year
Since you lost a loved one so dear
In such a short time, you've lost your husband and your son
A terrible loss to bear for anyone
I know if we could have one wish at our command
We would change what happened with the wave of a hand
But, you know that Kevin is gone, that is a, finality
But, he remains alive in memory, that is a reality
I know your heart is heavy, but it has been your strong belief
In God, and your faith in Him, that has eased your grief
I too lost a son, it was so suddenly
I felt my whole world had come crashing down upon me
I prayed to God to give me the words to say
To a friend who was remembering her son today
Betty my friend, I share your hurt and your pain
But, God promised us Sunshine, after the Rain
God said "death is not and ending
But an Afterlife, the start of a new beginning"
Kevin made an impact on all those that he met
Leaving you with wonderful memories, you will never forget
I feel Kevin would say to you, "one day we will be together
But until that day, remember, I LOVE YOU MOTHER"

Written for my good friend, Betty Evans whose son was taken so quickly

Should I Worry??

I had never worried about getting sick
I never had to wonder about what Dr. to pick
I did however worry about the cost
If for some reason my insurance I lost
But, I was always assured that they would pay
If I should find myself in a hospital one day
Then suddenly, my Government said to me
You must now change your insurance company
Prior conditions right now some Doctors will not touch
But this new plan will and you will pay half as much
Well, I changed my plan, I did what they said
But the increase from Obama Care has put me in the red
You can keep your Dr. and present insurance I was told
This was repeated so often, it soon became old
Nothing they said was true, they lied to me
They say now I have to pay, so that others can get it free
So now, if I get sick and cannot afford to pay
For the medical treatment I may need right away
The only way now is under the Obama Care
But that is only if I will pay "my fair share"
Obama thought his fix was the ultimate cure
But for many, this one thing we all know for sure
We do not need big brother to help us pick and choose
Saying, taking it now or you will lose
If I choose Obama Care, for me it would be a loss
Financially I could not afford the cost
It was a hard pill to swallow, this Obama Care Pill
It was shoved down our throats making many of us ill
My Doctor used to say take an aspirin, go home, get some rest
Call me in the morning and we will run some tests
Now, they say, go somewhere else, I do not care where
But, wherever you go, you better have Obama Care

Someone was Messing with my Mind

I was doing the bars, having fun
Drinking beer, whiskey, and rum
I told God, I still have plenty of time
But then, someone started messing with my mind

I wanted to party, sleep in late
Not really worrying about my fate
But God had different plans for me, you see
I now know that God was watching over me

God said it was time I took a stand, your actions accounted for
Not for the past sins of which you also deplored
But for the present life you have begun to lead
Warning signs from me, you must now heed

It was God all along who was messing with me
And He would not give up until my mind He freed
From all the sins that had me bound
Thank you God for staying around

I am sorry you had to go into
Those places where I drank and acted the fool
No more doing the bars and making the scene
God forgave my sins, my slate is now clean

Speaking from the Heart

I do not know just where to start
So I guess I will just speak from the heart
I have the right to speak out too
About the things you are trying to do
I know that you will agree with me
That you also enjoy your right of being free
No one can come to your house at night
And tell you that you no longer have any rights
That you must now work for your Government
But you won't get paid, not one red cent
That we will now make millions for those who rule
And we have no voice in what we must do
Well, you are not doing what we elected you to be
You are creating a world that is your fantasy
Brave men and women have died for both me and you
So that all our dreams would one day come true
We know our country has both good and bad within
But we do not fantasize, or look the other way and pretend
We know that there is a lot of pain and sorrow
That comes with preserving our peace for tomorrow
To those who protest against our freedom, I am ashamed
When you protest against our country, do not do it in my name
Mr. President, you were our nominee
Chosen to lead us, guide us, and keep us free
We are called ONE NATION, and we are UNITED
This is not something that just one person decided
It is you who is allowing others to put our country to shame
And we no longer want to hear that someone else is to blame
It was you we trusted, we made you are choice
But we will not let you forget that America still has a voice
We are Americans, we are proud and we stand tall
United we will stand, we will not be divided and fall

Special Moments Mother

"Hello Mother", I had you again on my mind
And I know it was God, giving me a sign
I do not keep in touch with you as much as I should
I do not visit you as often as I wish I could
But the bond between us is always there
And Mother, I hope you know that I really care
You sacrificed so much to keep your family together
We are grateful, both myself and Ronnie, my brother
I know we could have eased some of problems you had
By refraining from the things that made you so sad
But you stood by us until we both got grown
Watching each of us get married, having children of our own
Mother, you never gave up, you never counted us out
Though at times, we know you must have had some doubts
You were a loving Mother who always seen us through
Always there for us whenever we needed you
Mother, though we are many miles away
I think about you each and every day
I love you Mother, please know that I do
Though I know the times I tell you are far to few
I am now by God's blessing, have become a Mother too
I pray to God to be a Mother, just like you

SPECIAL TRIBUTE

We know that we have only mentioned a few
Of the beloved followers of God that we all knew
They all worked hard in one way or another
But they all worked for God and with each other
To get God's Church built and to build it strong
Where we would all gather to lift our voices in praise and song
Their energy and work is still seen here
Keeping our doors open, year after year
We remember them as our faithful and our guiding light
Let us continue on, to see our church grow and to win the fight

IN LOVING MEMORY
Frank Huffman . . . . Faye Kennedy . . . . Martha Tate . . . . Lee
Heileman
Gerlene Heileman . . . . Minister Winnie Mae Springs . . .
Henry{Mack} Springs
Shirley McLeod . . . . David Gene McLeod . . . . Q.L. Evans . . . .
Teddy Beach
Sara Beach . . . Joseph C. Griffin . . . Kate Yarbrough . . . Allen{Tetsi}
Griffin . . . Earl Miles

Standing Together

There are so many things we all want to say
About what is happening, here in the U.S.A.
But, our Government does not want us to speak
They do not want us strong they want us to be weak
Even our freedom of religion they are trying to take from us
If we speak out, they tell us to "Hush"
Well, you can only silence someone for just so long
Before they hit back, twice as strong
We voted for a Government, President, House and Senate
Saying, "take care of We the People", and we meant it
But, some of you, with money and perks you got showered
Becoming obsessed with so much power
Equality means for all, not a minority or who you are
It is not the rich that made you the man of the hour
So, now it is time for us to take our Government back
Putting back a Government we can trust, something we now lack
And for the Immigrants that want to come here, just do it right
Ask us for a Visa or Citizenship do not challenge us to a fight
We welcome you here to work with us side by side
For as long as you are legal, your rights too cannot be denied
So let us all stand together, hand in hand
To once again, make our country, the PROMISED LAND

TAKING OUR COUNTRY BACK

Our Government has now become a Government of lies and secrecies
No longer keeping their promise to the people of transparencies
It seems they got caught up in the game of power
Wanting their perks for themselves, becoming the man of the hour
But, we voted for you because of your promise to us
To be the Government of we the people, and stay close in touch
Mr. President, it was not your color that put you in the White House
But, you made it Racial, whenever someone would call you out
Because if, on anything you did and someone would disagree
You would deny us freedom of speech, and that cannot be
Our leadership has failed, our Government has become slack
So now, the voters are going to take our Government back
So, be on notice that it will not be long
Before we take back our country, again United and Strong

Taking the Time

I wish we would take more time
To find a solution to a problem and not just whine
We should look to see what the problem is
Rather than say, it's not my problem, it must be his
I know you did it and now I am through
I want nothing more to do with it or you
If we could only sit down and talk things out
Try finding a solution that won't leave any doubt
If we could be honest and open and talk to each other
I think we would be surprised and soon discover
How much in common that we all had
And the problems were not really all that bad
Then a pat on the back, a shake of the hand
Saying "thank you", we came together . . . AMEN

MY TIME WITH GOD

I set aside a special time every day
To talk to my God and to pray
I would not allow anything to interfere
When my Praying time would come near
I would watch the clock, waiting for the time
When I would talk to God, telling Him what was on my mind
I would then hear a quiet voice say to me, "you know that I care
I too am waiting to hear your Prayer"
But after He listened to my Prayer today
He said "you now must listen to what I have to say"
"Why do you sit aside a special time each day with Me
When you know I am with you always, no matter your need"
Yes, I want you to have that special, quiet time
To spend with me and get peace of mind
But, the time you set aside should not always be
The only time you choose to talk to me
Prayer should be genuine and from the heart
From this, I never want you to part
You can call on me any time, just say, "God, I need you now"
Do not feel that you have to wait until your chosen time rolls around

THAT DAY WHEN

When our minds grow weary and our bodies tire
When we lose all hope, our dreams and desire
When we wish that our pain would sub come
Then that is the day our Lord Jesus will come

When we say, "I am ready to give in"
When we cry out, "God, I am lonely, I need a friend"
When we finally cry out, "Lord Jesus, please"
That is the day, God will say, "I heard you crying out to me"

That day my God heard me and He answered my call
That day He picked me up, He would not let me fall
That day He wrapped His arms around me and I heard Him say
"I have come to be with you, this is That Day

The Actors Who Would Be

I do not know just where to start
So, I will just speak to you from my heart
I have the right to speak out too
About all the things I see you do
I know that on one thing we all agree
Is that we all enjoy being free
Where no one comes to your home in the mid of the night
To abuse you and tell you that you have no rights
You however make millions in what you do
By pretending to be someone other than you
You can live out this so called fantasy
Because you live in a land that is free
But, this is not a fantasy world that we live in
For there is much evil, still with within
I pray everyday that we will have peace
I pray that all our wars would finally cease
When our people march, it is not for fame
Or hopes of getting another star in front of their name
But, when you gather, it becomes a game
And it puts our leaders and country to shame
You go over to the other side, our enemy
And downgrade our President and our country
You hope you will again make the headlines
But, a meeting with our leaders, you decline
My President was our nominee, to him I want to say
Mr. President, I am an American and I am with you all the way
Written when some of the actors marched in protest of the President's
decision to enter Iraq

155

The American Fool

You may think that you have clout
But all you have is, one big mouth
Just what role were you playing today
When you went to the enemy to have your say
Just what did you expect to see
When you looked into the eyes of the enemy
Seeing their smirk, instead of a smiling face
Well, I am sorry, but to us you are all a disgrace
It is not their people with whom we are at war
But, it is their leaders whom we abhor
They are ruthless they are killers who only want to rule
And they are laughing at you, The American Fool
They will capitalize on what you have done
And tell their people, "see, even Americans we have won"
You are putting a wedge between us all
By saying that our leadership is weak and beginning to fall
The money that it took and that you have spent
To go to the enemy and speak against our President
Could have been spent to help their needy and poor
And that action would have spoken and done much more
Whoever you are trying so hard to impress
I am having a very hard time trying to digest
But, if your portrayal is that of a "has been"
You get the Oscar, but, you lost, for you did not win

Written after Sean Penn went to Iraq to meet with Sadam

The Day After

I went to bed and when I awoke
I heard the news, California had spoke
Well, I hope that what they had to say
Won't come back to haunt them one day
Arnie will not be given a Movie script
Or have a director giving him is cue or tip
Like assuming the identity of someone he is told
He will take on, while playing out this role
Already he is telling the President
I need every penny I can get, every red cent
Mr. President, you must send it to me
To help our state to become debt free
I heard someone say, if this is all it took to help us
Then why did we have to get rid of Governor Davis?
I too find it all so very insane
All the monies you have spent on this campaign
I think it is really quite evident
That all the monies that was spent
Could have been used to help your state instead
And you help get you out of the Red
Arnie has money, money to burn
His smokes cost more than most people earn
His shoes and all his clothes, he does not deny
The cost, my, my, my, how the money does fly
I think that Washington wanted him in
Because he is rich, and yes, he is a Republican
So, given all of this, then I have no doubt
That our President, will indeed help your state out

Written after Arnie won the seat for Governor
In the California recall election
October 2003

The Day I Left

Today I fought back the tears of seeing someone I loved
Being laid to rest, but I knew he was going to be in Heaven above
I listened to the words being said about him that day
And yes, the tears flowed and I too began to pray
A peace then came over me, I do not know why
But, I felt God beside me, I felt at peace and could no longer cry
I then hugged everyone, I told them I loved them and I cared
Mother, you and I, a great big hug and kiss we both shared
My life has not been perfect, I've done things of which I am not
proud
But, I heard God say, "I had given you all that Heaven would allow"
God also knew that I was not good at saying good-by
And I truly feel that this is why
He chose that day to quickly and quietly step in
Because I found peace with God, I felt He had forgiven me of my sin
To my Mother, I know you will always carry me in your heart
No good-byes because we will never be apart
To all my children, grandchildren, and Irene, my wife
You were my love, the reason for my life
To my brothers, we remained close, always had a ball
Getting together, laughing and enjoying the memories we would
recall
Remember me, and remember I did not say good-bye
Because we will all be together again, one day in Heaven on High

KEVIN EVANS
KILLED SUDDENLY THE SAME DAY HE HELPED LAY TO
REST HIS COUSIN
EARL MILES

THE DAY IN THE LIFE OF A MOTHER

I have so many errands today to run
I am already tired, but, I have just begun
I must taxi my children off to school
Pick up some of their friends they said "a few"
Grocery shopping that is next on my list
Checking it twice, making sure there is nothing I missed
Then back home to do the laundry, clean and dust
That is on my list too, and that is a must
Okay, I'm done with that and just in time
Off to school to pick up the children, I hope just mine
They said that they had plans, not to be late
Because they did not have time to stand around and wait
Well, here I am back home
The children are gone, I am again alone
They said, "be back in time for supper, make it a surprise"
Works for me, I will just fix hamburgers and fries
The day is over, everyone has now settled in
I am now going to relax, soak in the tub and then
Rest and get ready for tomorrow, another day
And if anyone asks me why, I will simply say
Every day I am with, and can do for my family I discover
This is not work, I really love, being a Mother

The Party is Over

I used to spend money, like I had it to burn
But I was spending more than I would earn
I wanted all the things that money could buy
Doing whatever was needed, even if I had to lie
I did the parties, making all the scenes
Made sure that I was always seen
I wanted everyone to know my name
I was trying hard to be a part of those with wealth and fame
But one day, a tragedy made me begin to realize
That no amount of wealth mattered when one dies
That when you are buried the only thing that would go
Would be this body of flesh and yes, even my soul
Well, the party is over for me my friend
Being seen in the nightlife scene will now end
I will still be making the scene
But this time, I will be a part of God's Team
For the only place that I want name to be
Is in God's Book of Who's Who, His Book of Eternity

THE PATH GOD LAYS

God touches all our lives in so many ways
And with each, a different pat He lays
He tells us of an Eternal Life that will never end
But He does not force us to follow Him
He died for our sins, for God says we must forgive
And that through Him, we must all live
Winnie Mae was one of those
Who took the path she said for her, God had chose
She served him faithfully, in all she did
She said she was an open book, from God, nothing was hid
She had a wonderful marriage, children she truly adored
And she became God's chosen, who could ask for anything more?
She kept working, asking God to open another door
Because she kept wanting to do, more and more
Even when tired and her body became weak
It was praying to God, she got the answers she would seed
God told Winnie Mae that she had served Him well
She always would answer her calling, she never failed
We know her name is written in God's Heavenly Book
So sure that even God said, "I don't have to look"
A wonderful friend, faithful and true
WINNIE MAE . . . . we all loved you

The Second Time Around

God intended for us to find someone
And to each, their hearts would be won
To spend with them our lives and devotion
Enjoying our lives with great emotion

Though the times we are together here
Could be as little as a day, sometimes, many a year
Wonderful memories will be made, along with a family
To carry on life as God has meant it to be

But sometimes we feel that life deals us a blow
Leaving us with a feeling of having no place to go
Especially when loved ones we should loose
Leaving us wondering what path we now should choose

The path that we sometimes choose may be a little slow
And finding the path hard, we tend to say, LET IT GO
Are we wrong to want to find another?
And once again, a new life we begin to discover

Because our new life as we know it here
Is something that we should not fear
We should live it and enjoy each and every day
And learn to take care of whatever God sends our way

Yes, God says we were meant to show our Emotion
And to Him and our loved ones, show our Devotion
For two hearts/souls that have found someone
Was God's way of saying, "you were meant to be united again, as one

THE TIE THAT BINDS

When two people tie the Knot that binds
They must first have a meeting of the mind
Both should promise to Love, Honor and Obey
But give each other space, trying not get in each others way
Whenever you go through some stormy weather
Just remember what brought you both together
So if you get upset, even mad as a wet hen
Just shake it off and count to ten
Many couples married for over fifty years
Will look at each other and say "why am I still here?"
The answer is simple, because they still truly love each other
They remembered, it was love that first brought them together

TIME OUT

I felt like I about to lose it, out of control
So, I am letting every one know
That I have decided what I will do today
Like, stay at home, out of everyone's way
I will just look in the mirror if I am wanting some company
Who better to talk with now, but, you guessed it, ME
I will lock all my doors and upon them put a note
'GONE FISHING', I'm out in the boat
I need quiet time, I need to be alone
No t.v.'s, cells, or even a telephone
Now I can jump and holler, scream and yell
Say what I want, telling everyone to . . . well,
I want to work with others freely, not because you demand
I am taking me back, I hope everyone will understand

TO ALL MY FAMILY

I know that it has been almost a year
Since I left earth and those that I loved so dear
But, here, there is no such thing as time
While on earth, it is always on our mind
We do not know the time or even when
Our time on earth, will suddenly end
So it was that eventful day with me
When I unexpectedly left home and all of my family
I see your pain, your hurt, and so much crying
I see some of you giving up hope, not even trying
Trying to accept what happened, why I am no longer there
Even blaming God, saying that He did not care
God is a caring God who has let you take a quick glance
At your lives, and is giving you a second chance
He says you must love one another, do all that you can
Even saying, I forgive you and I do understand
You must stay right with God, living your life
Free of hatred, doubts and so much strife
It is only then that when all of this has ceased
That you will find God and an inner peace
Do not cry for me, for I am in a better place
No longer a part of the Human Race
I have met some of my friends, and my family
My Father Q.L., cousin Earl, and even Uncle J.C.
We are all looking forward to the day when
We will be reunited and together once again
And when those Pearly Gates begin to open wide
We'll be waiting, saying Welcome, please come inside

Written to the family and loved ones of Kevin Evans
After his sudden passing

To all you terrorist who persist
Know that we will not desist
We will fight you on the land, the air, the sea
For that is what Freedom means to me
The end for you is very near
For we will not live in constant fear
We will not run and hide from you
Our colors are not yellow, they are
    RED—WHITE—and—BLUE

        These rights we will defend
         Until the very end

        We must eliminate the fear of terror
        There is no more room for error

<u>To My Family</u>

This was to have been the beginning of a new year
Our coming together as a family and being of good cheer
Things took a sudden change, today I see you all crying and sad
But I want you all to remember the good times that we had
Remember the times we gathered together, one big happy family
These times cannot be forgotten, they will remain as a memory
I want you to also know that it was your love that helped me sustain
Kept me able to bear my tragedies, my sickness and my pain
I am at peace now, and my body is again whole
I will now walk with the Angels on Heaven's Streets of Gold
Remember that we must all love one another
Trust in God and know, one day we will be together
God said that I now had Eternal Life, never ending
But for my loved ones on earth, each day for them is now a new
beginning
I did not leave you when I left with Jesus that day
He promised I would always be with you, for Heaven's not far away
I told God, "thank you for the family I loved and adored"
God said, "you are welcome my child, but, I loved your more"

**TO ALL THE FAMILY OF MY WONDERFUL FRIEND
MARY ANN MANN FARRELL**

To My Family

Sometimes we get so caught up in our own tears and pain
That we only count ours losses and not our gains
Today, I fought back the tears of seeing someone I loved
Being laid to rest, being taken to Heaven above
Suddenly I felt a peace come over me
I felt God was standing close, and I felt free
I felt God had forgiven me also of my sins
And then He quickly and quietly stepped in
Mother, you were my world, to me you meant so much
Always there when needed with a Mother's tender touch
Only you were able to put up with someone like me
Maybe because I was your youngest, your loving son of three
To my brothers and friends, I ask you all to stay strong
Keep your faith in God even when things seem to go wrong
To my wife, I loved you and now it is up to you
To stay strong for our children and grandchildren, they need you too
Bonita, my cousin and also my dear friend
Please know that you did not cause my life to end
No one knows when or why or even who God will choose
He does not send ahead, sending out little clues
For when it is our time to go
Sometimes, like me, it will be quick, one never knows
You had just come from seeing your only brother laid to rest
When God laid upon you another test
Know God at times will at times place upon us pain and sorrow
Not to punish us but to make us stronger for tomorrow
I believe that God has placed a test upon all of my family
You all need to now come together in love, living in peace and
harmony
So, I leave this, with all of you this, my one last Prayer
Until we all meet again one day with the Man upstairs

**KEVIN EVANS A MOTORCYCLE ACCIDENT/
SAME DAY AS HIS COUSIN'S FUNERAL**

Tribute to my Friends

I decided that while I still had the time
I would pay tribute, not to me, but to friends of mine
I wanted them all to know
Just how much I loved and appreciated them so
Each one of you entered my life for different reasons
Making my life so very Blessed and so pleasin'
I thank God for having placed my friends, so very many
Enemies I hope were few, I am sorry if I made any
You all helped me in so many ways
You helped me get through many of my bad days
And when I would ask for your Prayers
My friends, you came out from everywhere
There are not enough words that can be written or said
That can be expressed, words I want to say, not have them read
Yes, I know you will gather round me when I have passed
I know you will cry and say, she had a good life while it did last
But, I won't be around to hear these words said
Or hear my Eulogy as it is being read
My friends, I know that you will gather and you will grieve
I know that you will give comfort also to my family
Even though I have gone on, I know I can still depend
On you being there for my family, cause you are still my friend
Yes, I just wanted to see and once more tell all of you
Thank you for all you have done for me and will continue to do
I truly believe that friends cannot be bought or rented
But are a Blessing sent from Heaven as God had intended

Thank you all my friends . . . my feelings to you I wanted to describe
I know that we will one day be together again, on the other side

VOICES

Well here it is, Monday night
And I just decided I would write
About the things that are coming to my mind
It does not matter if the words do not rhyme
It seems as though every time I hear a voice
I start to do it, I hear another saying, you have a choice
When someone says something that confuses me
Another voice says, "not all is as it seems to be
I sometimes wonder why things are happening, the way they are
Then I hear a voice saying, "you have come so far
Do not let others take you down
When at last, Jesus you have found"
I think about my life a year ago
And how I felt my life had become so low
That there was no need for me to live, I had no one
Then I heard a voice saying, "I gave to you my Son"
Though at times, things still give me grief and pain
This voice keeps telling me to just look at what I have gained
I still do not understand fully what is happening to me
But I will keep doing whatever it is that God wants me to be
So, if you look for me, I can be found
Standing here on this higher ground
Just waiting to hear the voice of Jesus say
"Keep your feet planted, for I will be back one day"
The grounds are high and solid, not soft like clay
My feet are firmly planted, I will not stray
For I now know that Satan no longer has me bound
Since God lifted me and placed me on a Higher Ground

WE BELIEVE

If you want to live in America, the good OLD USA
We believe there are rules that you must obey
If you come here because you wanted to belong
We believe you should obey our laws, not go wrong
We also believe that if you break our laws, you should go back
We do not believe in bowing down or giving any slack
We believe that many immigrants who are crossing our border
Are doing so, just to cause trouble and disorder
You then try to take our jobs by using our Justice Powers
You try taking away whatever is ours
We believe our Government is so busy trying to appease
All the ones who are trying to slip into our country
Your country does nothing to solve the problem, but when they're in
need
They turn to us, the land of the Free
We believe in justice, in helping our fellow man
We believe they too deserve to take a stand
To better their lives, their futures to enhance
Because we believe that everyone deserves a chance
But, we also believe that we have the right
To defend our country from all those who might
Cross over our borders, on to our land with only one thing in mind
To cause dissention, hatred, and mistrust in mankind
But, it will not work here, for our America is strong
We will find you and send you back to where you belong
We want everyone to know by the powers that be
We are the UNITED STATES of AMERICA . . . WE BELIEVE

We're the Best

Where has the time gone?
It just does not seem to have been that long
Since we all sat together in our class
Dreaming of the future, not of the past
We shared our secrets with other class mates
Getting involved in all our class debates
Voting for the cutest boy or girl, our special contest
Yes, our class was special, we were indeed the best
Here we all are again sitting with the class who cared
Talking of our past and memories that we again will share
Yes, still together, just slowed down, no longer in a rush
Our class, still the very best, we have not lost our touch

Class of "55"

What Does a Medal Cost?

What is all this ado over the Swits?
Are they commanded by a bunch of Twits?
When they said their ships all set sail
They were right, and their brains went as well
You all fought for us, you all were brave
You all had one goal, our country to save
You stood together, everyone side by side
Something none of you has ever denied
Many years later, you were all together again
But you are divided, some of you will lose, some will win
Some of you are fighting over medals, given and worn upon your
chest
Medals given to and worn, only by America's best
Have you forgotten about all those who fought and died
Or all the tears that you and all America cried?
They were acknowledged as Americas' best
But all they got, was dirt thrown upon their chests
Why did you not speak out before you got home
If you had a problem with one of your own
For once a medal is given, right or wrong
To the person it is given, it will now belong
So, why don't you lay Anchor and come back aboard
And fight for the peace that we are all still fighting for
You are now waging a "no win situation"
That is never part of any duty station
Remember, United we will stand, but, Divided we will fall
America is All for one and One for all

**Written regarding the election smears by the Swits on Candidate
John Kerry who was part of
Their group during the Viet Nam war and had received a medal
8-28-04**

What If

What if the world were flat, not round?
What if, you first, I had found?
What if the Sun was not hot, but cold?
What if we stayed young and never grew old?
I wish I could in some way, change the world
I wish a new book I could unfurl
I wish the Sun with its' warmth would keep me embraced
I wish my getting older, I never had to face
But, I cannot change the tides of time
I cannot wish for something that is not mine
I cannot pretend that there is another
I cannot pretend that you are my lover
God gave me a mind with which I can dream
But also to face reality, not dream of things that seem
In reality, we both know these facts to be true
A loving friendship is all we have, between me and you
So, I can wish, but I cannot change, only say, "what if"?
Our time and the circumstance may one day shift
Until then, even though we are miles apart
We will still be together, but only in our heart

**SOMETIMES A LOVE LOST CAN ONE DAY BE FOUND
UNTIL THEN, ONLY IN YOUR HEART CAN YOU DARE TO
DREAM**

Who is She?

She keeps busy in lots of ways
Sometimes, even wishing she had more days
She works so hard, she is always in so much demand
That she asks God to help her out as much as He can
She is active in all our Church deeds
Helping us to plant and sow God's seeds
Seeds that will help our Church to really grow
And she does it for God, not for show
She has put us all together, no, not in print
Can you name her?, here, I will give you a hint
She took a string of yarn, made a blanket of love
Working for hours with God's guidance from above
When she was finished God smiled, saying "well done"
Mother of my Shepherd, my appointed one
In this blanket you have joined us all as one
Mother, Father, sister, brother, daughter and son

++++THE SHEEP AND THE BLANKET BOTH HAVE A
FOLD
AND BOTH CAN BE UNRAVELED IF ONE IS NOT TOLD
THAT IF THE BLANKET BEGINS TO FRAY OR THE SHEEP
BEGIN TO STRAY
THEN THE KNITTER MUST KNIT AND THE SHEPHERD
MUST PRAY++++

With This Ring

Today, I know the Angels in Heaven will sing
As we stand before God and pledge our love with this ring
This ring is a symbol of our love for each other
We know it was God who brought us together
Years of happiness we know God will give to us
As long as it is with each other and in God we place our trust
To all our family and friends who showed how much they care
By being with us today, being a part of this love we share
Thank you for sharing in the exchange of our Wedding Vow
Being united and joined together, forever, beginning now

Mr. & Mrs. Bobby Grimsley
June 24, 2012

ZACK

I know that it has been almost a year
Since I left the family that I loved so dear
But, God did not say that you should put aside
Memories of a loved one who has "died"
But that we should hold them forever in our heart
Go on with our lives, each generation becomes a new start
You must take care of yourself and each other, this to you I say
Though I have moved on, God has given to you another day
Son, I want you to take pride in all that you do
Because the way you live your life will always reflect on you
Zack, not only were you my son, you were also my best friend
Always there for me when needed, embracing me right up to the end
Son, I want you to stand firm in all that you do and believe
So that one day, God's promise to you, you will one day receive
We can still have talks, in spirit to man, but one on one
I will hear you and we in that moment we will again be like
Father/Son

ZACK
**YOUR FATHER LOVED YOU VERY MUCH AND THOUGH
THE PAIN FOR YOU OF SEEING YOUR FATHER FOR THE
LAST TIME, HOLDING HIM WILL FOREVER BE A PART
OF YOUR MEMORY, YOUR FATHER SAYS YOU MUST
LET IT GO AND KNOW THAT IT GAVE HIM COMFORT
IN KNOWING THAT YOU WERE THERE, AND HE DID
KNOW . . . . THE HEART AND MIND ARE A COMPLEX
THING AND IT CAN HELP US OR BREAK US . . . WE
CANNOT DWELL ON THE PAST BUT MOVE FORWARD,
WORK FOR THE FUTURE OF YOURSELF, YOUR FAMILY,
YOUR CHILDREN, THE NEXT GENERATION . . . LET
OUR LOVED ONES BE PROUD OF US . . . LET THE NEXT
GENERATION BE ONE THAT WILL MEMORIES OF
LOVE . . . IT IS THEN THAT WE KNOW WE MADE IT
GOD BLESS**

About the Author

My name is Marlene Wheeler Scott and I live in Santee, S.C.

I was born in Kentucky, but I grew up and graduated in a little farming town called Camden, Ohio . . . After graduation joined the Navy where I met and married My husband, also in the U.S.N., living mostly in Charleston, S.C . . . We had four children, three sons and a daughter, nine grandchildren and six great grandchildren and we have been married for fifty six years

My second son, Mark, passed away suddenly and unexpectedly leaving a deep void in so many of our lives, especially in mine as I thought my life too had ended . . . I started writing to him after he passed, talking to him, asking him questions, all in poem that came from my heart of how I felt, how I thought he had felt, and even to things I felt he would have said to me and his loved ones. Writing seemed to bring me closer to him and gave me more of an understanding about how precious life is and I became more aware that the time God gives us with our loved ones is indeed God's gift to us and we should give thanks to God every day for that Blessing

A few months after his passing, we moved to a small town, Santee, S.C. where I met a friend, Shirley McLeod who took me to this small church on the lake, Lakeside Outreach Ministries where I found love, peace and understanding and God . . . I soon met others with pain and suffering from the loss of loved ones, who also was looking for answers . . . It was then I truly began writing

I began writing poems for others who had experienced the loss of a loved one, or was having spiritual, emotional, or health problems . . . my poems seemed to connect with them, giving them peace and understanding, sometimes, it was as if their loved ones were giving me words to write and give to their loved ones here and my writing for them also brought me closer to my son . . . God showed me that death does not separate us, it brings us closer together . . . I know without God, my family and my church, my poems would never have been, for it was God who gave me these words

I do want to say also that while writing the Eulogy for my son, I put a period at the end of a sentence, and suddenly a voice told me that putting a period at the end of a sentence meant it was the end, the sentence was over, so I do not put periods at the end of any sentence I write, because then these words can go on and on and on . . . just like even in death, life goes one